Managing Special Educational Needs

A practical guide for primary and secondary schools

Dr. Suanne Gibson completed her PhD 'Middle management and the role of the SENCO, a study of management in practice' at Oxford Brookes University 2002. She currently works as senior lecturer and Programme Director, BA Education Studies Degree, University of Plymouth.

Professor Sonia Blandford is currently Dean of Education at Canterbury Christ Church University College. She has published widely on Education Management and Learning and Teaching.

Managing Special Educational Needs

A practical guide for primary and secondary schools

Suanne Gibson and Sonia Blandford

P·C·P

Paul Chapman
Publishing

Paul Chapman Publishing
A SAGE Publications Company
1 Oliver's Yard
55 City Road
London EC1Y 1SP

SAGE Publications Inc
2455 Teller Road
Thousand Oaks, California 91320

SAGE Publications India Pvt Ltd
B-42, Panchsheel Enclave
Post Box 4109
New Delhi 110 017

Library of Congress Control Number: 2004116992

A catalogue record for this book is available from the British Library

ISBN 1-4129-0302-5
ISBN 1-4129-0303-3 (pbk)

Typeset by Pantek Arts Ltd, Maidstone, Kent
Printed in Great Britain by Cromwell Press, Trowbridge, Wilts

Dedication

To Mum and Dad, my first teachers still happy to listen, my students and colleagues for the energy and inspiration.

To Charlie, Bethany and Mia who make these words real.

Contents

Acknowledgements

The approach to the writing of this book has been to consult interested and valued practitioners and academics. Thanks go to the Centre for Enabling Learning, Canterbury Christ Church University College. Thanks also to Dr Sacha Powell, Department of Educational Research, Canterbury Christ Church University College; Susan Soan, Department of Professional Development, Canterbury Christ Church University College; and Pat Sikes, School of Education, University of Sheffield.

The authors are also grateful to Kim Blanning for permission to reproduce material in this book.

Glossary

ATL	Association of Teachers and Lecturers
AUP	Acknowledge Understand and Provide
AWCEBD	Association of Workers for Children with Emotional and Behavioural Difficulties
AWPU	Age Weighted Pupil Unit
BCODP	British Council of Disabled People
BECTA	British Educational Communications and Technology Agency
BESD	Behavioural, Emotional and Social Difficulties
BEST	Behaviour and Education Support Team
CFSC	Child and Family Support Centre
CMC	Community Music Centre
CoP	Code of Practice
CPD	Continuing Professional Development
CSIE	Centre for Studies on Inclusive Education
DDA	Disability Discrimination Act
DES	Department of Education and Science
DfE	Department for Education
DfEE	Department for Education and Employment
DfES	Department for Education and Skills
DRC	Disability Rights Commission
EP	Educational Psychologist
ERA	Education Reform Act
EWO	Education Welfare Officer
EWS	Education Welfare Service
FNN	Family Nurturing Network
GTC	General Teaching Council
HEI	Higher Education Institution
ICT	Information Communication Technology

IEP	Individual Education Plan
IMC	International Music Centre
INSET	In-Service Education and Training
IPT	Inclusion Policy Team
ISB	Individual Schools Budget
ITE	Initial Teacher Education
LEA	Local Education Authority
LMS	Local Management of Schools
LSC	Learning and Skills Council
MLD	Moderate Learning Difficulties
NAHT	National Association of Head Teachers
NCSL	National College for School Leadership
NPBEA	National Policy Board for Educational Administration
NQT	Newly Qualified Teachers
OfSTED	Office for Standards in Education
PC	Politically Correct
PLASC	Pupil Level Annual Schools Census
PMLD	Profound and Multiple Learning Difficulties
PTA	Parent–Teacher Association
SAD	Sisters Against Disability
SAT	Standard Assessment Test
SDP	Self-development Planning
SEN	Special Educational Needs
SENCO	Special Educational Needs Co-ordinator
SENDA	SEN and Disability Act
SMART	Specific, Measurable, Attainable, Relevant and Time-limited
SSD	Social Services Department
TA	Teaching Assistant
TQM	Total Quality Management
TTA	Teacher Training Agency
UNESCO	United Nations Educational, Scientific and Cultural Organisation
UPIAS	Union of the Physically Impaired Against Segregation
VAK	Visual, Auditory, Kinaesthetic

Prologue

Please accept and value our children (and ourselves as families) as we are.

Please celebrate difference.

Please try and accept our children as children first. Don't attach labels to them unless you mean to do something.

Please recognise your power over our lives. We live with the consequences of your opinions and decisions.

Please understand the stress many families are under. The cancelled appointment, the waiting list no one gets to the top of, all the discussions about resources – it's our lives you're talking about.

Do recognise that sometimes we are right. Please believe us and listen to what we know that we and our child need.

Sometimes we are tired and depressed. Please value us as caring and committed families and try to go on working with us.

Russell (1997, p. 79)

Preface

The purpose of this book is to provide those involved in the delivery and management of mainstream primary and secondary education with guidance, advice and practical examples on managing special educational needs (SEN). The focus is on the management of special educational needs within mainstream settings. In providing the reader with a flavour of what is to come, the authors would like to make their position with regards 'inclusion' and 'inclusive schooling' known. Inclusion is taken to mean 'to be included', which runs counter to those who view inclusive schooling in a limited way which leads to restriction in our practices. Inclusive schooling is not just about providing full access to education for children labelled with special educational needs; inclusive schooling means providing all children, regardless of race, language, disability, class and geographical location, with equitable and effective education that responds to their needs as learners. As Slee (2001, p. 116) comments:

> *Inclusive schooling is a greater challenge than is implied. ... in the technical attempts to mobilise sufficient resources to contain disabled children in incrementally modified classrooms.*

Croll and Moses (1998) and Rosenthal (2001) consider that inclusive schooling demands practitioners, researchers and academics to critically engage with what constitutes effective education for all. This requires the individual to determine their views, values and attitudes towards those perceived to be different, as Rosenthal (2001, p. 385) states:

> *... to address discrimination and education for all move towards more fully promoting the inclusion agenda, we have to provide regular meaningful dialogues between pupils and teachers, and we have to individually examine and adjust our own less-social perceptions, values and actions. All of us need to experience and hear each other's points of view, and the differences between us have to be acknowledged and explored, rather than ignored and denied.*

As such, this book addresses one specific group of pupils for whom equitable and effective education still seems out of reach; those children considered to have SEN; those who are playing the role of the 'other' in many parts of our mainstream education system. The book considers contemporary research focusing on theory and practice that relates to inclusive education and special educational needs.

Schools are now central to the development of the knowledge society; a society which is built on trust and transparency. Inclusion of all pupils in the creation of knowledge is at the heart of a value-led school that embraces actions of the learning community.

As inclusion is about diversity, celebration and the facilitation of diversity, this book will provide the practitioner with a framework from which such professional judgement and reflective practice can grow, enabling them to provide an effective learning environment for all pupils.

In summary, the authors' aim is to provide the reader with a body of knowledge and practice that informs critical engagement with contemporary issues and practices relating to the management of the provision of inclusive education for pupils with SEN. It is hoped that in so doing the authors will encourage growth in thought and scope of practice relating to inclusion and the management of special educational needs in mainstream primary and secondary education.

Special Educational Needs

CHAPTER 1: KEY QUESTIONS TO BE CONSIDERED
■ What are the origins of special educational needs (SEN)?
■ How were pupils with SEN educated in the nineteenth and twentieth centuries?
■ Why and how did provision change?
■ How have practices since the late nineteenth century influenced current provision?

Introduction

A framework for the management of inclusion and special educational needs (SEN) requires an understanding of context. This chapter provides an historic overview of the education of pupils deemed as having special educational needs in England and Wales from the late nineteenth century. This history focuses on government acts and committee reports that legislate and inform the development of a separate education for pupils with various disabilities and SEN. It also provides a critical insight into particular societal influences, connecting them to developments within the education system. Models of disability are considered which provide insights into how perceptions of, and provision for, disability had a significant bearing on the development of a separate education system for pupils with SEN.

This chapter will give practitioners a clearer knowledge and understanding of the concept and context of SEN in mainstream education from its origins as determined by the initial aims and objectives of its architects. Within this historical context, this chapter will:

■ provide insight on how practitioners perceive and understand special educational needs

■ consider how this subsequently impacts on practice

■ consider the use of language, indicating how this reflects practitioners' values and attitudes.

1

In order to understand these aims it is imperative the concept of SEN be addressed and its perception as an overused acronym in society and education understood. To trace its development, the chapter is divided into two sections:

- Section One: The education of children with disabilities from 1870 until 1970

- Section Two: The emergence of SEN

Tables 1.1, 1.2 and 1.3 provide a summary of the provision for children with disabilities and SEN in the education system of England and Wales from 1870 to 2004 separated into three periods:

- Medical model of disability and segregation (1870–1970)

- Needs model of disability and integration (1971–1989)

- Social model of disability and inclusion (detailed in Chapter 2).

It must be understood that these three models of disability continue to exert an influence upon educational policies and practices in mainstream education in England and Wales. The authors believe that it is the social model that promotes practices of inclusion.

Table 1.1 Medical model of disability and segregation (1870–1970)

1870 Foster's Elementary Education Act
Elementary education for all pupils 5–13.

1880 Education Act
Compulsory for all pupils to attend school with the exception of the 'uneducable'.

1893 Elementary Education Act
Raised the school leaving age to 11.

1893 Elementary Education Blind and Deaf Children Act
Enabled the provision of special schools for blind and deaf children.

1899 Education Act
Set up special schools to run distinct from mainstream schools for the benefit of those pupils for whom withdrawal classes in mainstream were not deemed effective.

1913 Education Act
Raised the school leaving age to 14.

1921 Education Act
Five categories were devised for those children deemed having a 'handicap' and therefore 'defective'. They were provided with a placement via the Health Authority. These categories were: blind, deaf, mentally defective, physically defective and epileptic. There was also reference made to the 'imbecile'.

1944 Education Act

Leaving age rose from 15 to 16. Board of Education now a Ministry of Education co-ordinating all Local Education Authorities (LEAs). Ten categories of handicap identified. 'Severely subnormal' remained the responsibility of Health Authority.

1970 Education (Handicapped Children) Act

Concept of 'uneducable' removed. Severely subnormal pupils moved from Health Authority remit to education, i.e. junior occupational centres became special schools.

Table 1.2 Needs model of disability and integration (1971–1989)

1976 Education Act

Abolished selection by ability for secondary education.

1978 Warnock Report

Removed all categories of handicap and replaced them with a spectrum of SEN. Special education provision recommended beginning as early as possible. Greater parental involvement encouraged. A five-stage recognition and assessment of needs established.

1981 Education Act 'Special Educational Needs'

Established Warnock's recommendations. Categories of handicap abolished and placed onto new SEN five-stage spectrum of need.

1988 Education Reform Act (ERA)

National Curriculum established. All pupils including those in special schools entitled to access National Curriculum.

Table 1.3 Social model of disability and inclusion (detailed in Chapter 2)

1993 Education Act

Aimed to increase schools' quality, diversity, autonomy and accountability and extend parental choice. Policy promoted the education of children with SEN in mainstream schools where and when possible. Class teachers responsible for SEN in early stages.

1994 Code of Practice on the Identification and Assessment of Special Educational Needs

The role of the Special Educational Needs Co-ordinator (SENCO) made statutory; all schools have a SENCO whose job is to co-ordinate provision for pupils with SEN.

1995 Disability Discrimination Act (DDA)

It became unlawful to discriminate against disabled persons in connection with employment, the provision of goods, facilities and services or the disposal or management of premises.

1997 Circular 10/97: Requirements for Courses of Initial Teacher Training
Qualified teacher status to include understanding how learning is affected by pupils' physical, intellectual, emotional and social development.

1997 Green Paper: Excellence for All Children
Focused on increasing inclusion and emphasised collaborative practice between special and mainstream sectors.

1998 White Paper: Meeting Special Educational Needs: A Programme of Action
Following the setting up of the National Advisory Group on Special Educational Needs and nation-wide consultancy on the 1994 Code of Practice (CoP), this paper formed the basis from which a revised CoP emerged.

2001 The Code of Practice for Special Educational Needs
The revised CoP suggested the management role of SENCO be shared in a team. It also stated that parents and pupils be included in assessment and review stages.

2001 SEN and Disability Act (SENDA)
New duties extending the 1995 DDA to cover every aspect of education. The Act amended the DDA inserting a new Part IV to prevent discrimination against disabled people accessing education. The duties make it unlawful to discriminate against pupils on the basis of their disability in all aspects of school life.

2002 Special Educational Needs Report
This report highlighted that children were waiting too long to have needs assessed and many special schools were feeling uncertain as to their future role. It also noted that LEAs and Health Authorities varied in their levels of support available to families.

2003 Every Child Matters
The government strategy for multi-agency collaborative support for all pupils.

2004 Barriers to Inclusion
The government's strategy for SEN containing a programme for sustained action reiterating the need for the whole school community including parents, guardians, pupils, the voluntary, health and social services working together in order to meet the needs of all pupils.

Section One: Education of children with disabilities (1870–1970)

Foster's 1870 Act for compulsory elementary education established nation-wide compulsory elementary education for pupils aged 5–13, and was the first legislation to have an impact on children with a range of physical and mental disabilities. Depending on the severity of need, these children were normally institutionalised with the Health Department as their guardians. Interestingly, Arnold (1964) and Hurt (1988) commented on the complaints made by teachers following the 1870 Act; their major concern being that certain pupils were uneducable and in their view had no place in the education system.

In 1889 the government established the Egerton Committee, which was tasked with assessing the problem of uneducable pupils and establishing how widespread were such cases. There followed the 1893 Elementary Education Act, which provided for pupils with sensory difficulties, i.e. blind and deaf children.

The Sharpe Committee was set up in 1898 in response to increasing pressure made on government by teachers and the medical profession to make mandatory and effective provision for pupils with disabilities other than sensory difficulties. The most significant recommendation was the establishment of special schools for those pupils for whom withdrawal classes in mainstream schools were ineffective. The subsequent 1899 Education Act incorporated some of the committee's recommendations, in particular that special schools should be set up to run distinct from mainstream schools. The authority for implementing the Act was left to local government, resulting in diversified change and development at the local level (Potts, 1982).

Hegarty (1987) noted that government policy regarding provision for the disabled learner became more focused when the 1913 Education Act for defective and epileptic children was introduced. This Act was an outcome of Royal Commission reports published in 1899 and 1908.

KEY QUESTIONS
■ What practices did policy promote regarding the education of children with disability in the nineteenth century?
■ In what ways do you consider that policy and practice toward the education of children with disability has changed?

The 1921 Education Act instituted five categories for those children deemed to have a handicap and therefore to be defective or unable to access a mainstream education. It also made reference to the imbecile, deemed to be uneducable. Uneducable children of compulsory school age remained under the guardianship of the Health Department accommodated in specialist hospitals or wards.

Following the 1921 Act, Burt and Schonell, whose theories were based upon that of eugenics and psychometrics, influenced policy makers in providing for pupils who had disabilities affecting learning potential (learning difficulties). Burt (1921, 1935) identified some 15 per cent of children as having learning difficulties thus placing them at a disadvantage in mainstream education. Schonell (1924) noted that 17 per cent of pupils were found within the 'disadvantaged category' or as having learning difficulties. Burt (1921) suggested there were three groups within the disadvantaged category: subnormal intelligence, mentally dull, and inferior intelligence. Schonell (1924) also identified three groups of disadvantaged children: dull, backward and retarded. Significantly Burt and Schonell concluded that the most effective method for educating such pupils was in a segregated environment. Specifically, Schonell advocated the use of special schools for the backward and retarded. For the dull group the use of small group withdrawal sessions was advised which, it was argued, would enable the pupil to eventually return to a mainstream classroom.

Early educational theories were based upon three models for the effective provision of SEN: deficiency, within-child and medical (Lindsay and Thompson, 1997). These models stem from a single understanding that segregation, and in certain cases the child's placement in special schools or hospitalised institutions, must occur to provide effectively for SEN. The medical model promotes a deficit view of the learner, i.e. that the cause of SEN lies solely with the child, hence the child is deficient and external factors are not considered causal. Sandow (1994, p. 3) provides a succinct definition of this perception of disability with its advocating of segregated education:

> *The medical model is the most commonly cited explanation of special educational needs. The doctor in the nineteenth century was subject to ideas about causality which was never perceived as social but always hereditary ... the doctor sought only to prevent disability.*

Butler's 1944 Education Act asserted that the most effective method of teaching those with a handicap was to continue with the establishment of special schools and further segregation after the age of eleven into secondary, technical or grammar depending on intellect. Tilstone et al. (1998, p. 106) noted that the tri-partite system of education with primary, secondary and further education provided for all except those deemed 'uneducable'. The Act increased the initial five categories to ten, identified as: blind, partially sighted, deaf, partially deaf, delicate, educationally subnormal, epileptic, maladjusted, physically handicapped and speech defects.

KEY QUESTIONS

■ How has the medical model informed the practice of education professionals?

■ How have contemporary attitudes and understandings of social justice and inclusion challenged these practices?

Oliver (1998, p. 13) considered that government educational policy between 1944 and 1979 was based upon the notion of humanitarianism, 'the social administrative approach to social welfare'. Barton and Tomlinson (1984) also believed that the approach to educating children with disabilities post 1945 was 'benevolent humanitarianism'; in practice this is translated as doing good to individual children.

In 1963 the Newsom Report, which focused on the provision within secondary modern schools, identified a lack of consistency in provision across England and Wales. The report found that there was only provision for the disabled learner where there was support of head teachers and individual school management teams rather than any local authority policy or directive.

At this time, an important influence was the materialist perspective which viewed disability as a form of exclusion created and maintained by the economic system. Abberley (1987, p. 10), an exponent of this view, stated:

... the main and consistent beneficiary [of exclusion] must be identified as the present social order, or more accurately, capitalism.

During this period, Marxist ideologies gathered momentum and importance. Abberley (1987) and Slee (1998) condemned segregated education provision as being part of government's wider aims to achieve order and stability through social control. Young people not deemed as economically useful to the furtherance of the state were kept out of the way, i.e. segregated. In contrast, pluralists asserted that all people, regardless of who or what they were, had a right to a full and equitable life. Clearly with Local Education Authorities (LEAs) and schools, the practice of promoting segregation meant that this right was infringed.

During in the 1960s, disability rights groups emerged to counter the materialist discourse (Thomas, 1997). Part of this ideology was that effective provision for children with disabilities could, and should, be found within mainstream education. These views contributed to the emergence of new policy concerning the integration of pupils with SEN.

These developments ran parallel to the evolving debate on comprehensive schooling. The government (DES, 1965) introduced the comprehensive system in England, leading to a change in the way in which mainstream education was structured. Musgrave (1968) reported on the benefits of the comprehensive model for all pupils and teaching staff and suggested that such a system would provide benefits for pupils with disabilities. However, since 1965, there has been much debate questioning the benefits of the comprehensive model, particularly with regard to the education of pupils with disabilities (Stakes and Hornby, 1997).

Following the introduction of comprehensive schools, in line with other societal movements, the 1970 Education (Handicapped Children) Act integrated those formerly referred to as imbeciles into a special education setting within mainstream schools. This resulted in the transfer of responsibility for severely handicapped children from the Department of Health to the Department of Education and Science (DES) with junior occupational centres being renamed and developed as special schools. These new special schools were managed by LEAs.

As a consequence of the 1970 Education Act, a new genre of researchers and educators emerged to provide and comment on the educational needs of those formally referred to as uneducable. The DES established a committee to address national provision for pupils with disabilities in mainstream settings. The 1971 report, *Slow Learners in Secondary Schools* (DES, 1971), found that only one third of secondary schools made any provision for the slowest pupils who seem to have been given less than their fair share of consideration.

Educationalists were more critical; Smedley (1974, p. 118) described the general attitude towards pupils with SEN as *ambivalent* while Bell (1970, p. viii) described it as *inadequate with overall planning being non-existent*. Smedley (1974) detailed several features of the system including a lack of continuity between primary and secondary stages and the burden resting on the individual teacher and a lack of relevant teacher training. Westwood (1975, p. 157) described the secondary school setting as 'the graveyard of human potential for the non-academic child ... the overall situation was tantamount to a national scandal'.

A further example of the difficulties associated with provision for children with SEN in the mainstream sector was the variety of labels used in government documentation. Tomlinson (1982) provides an analysis of the changes to the naming of such pupils in official documentation:

- Schonell (1924) and Burt (1937) – retarded

- 1944 Education Act – backward

- Tansley and Culliford (1960) – slow learners

- Westwood (1975) – less able.

In practice, the variety of labels used added to the difficulties of managing special educational needs across England and Wales coherently. Writing on the overall effect of pupils requiring special help in the mainstream school, Brennan (1971, pp. 7–10) commented that their educational future was at the mercy of completely fortuitous circumstances dependent on LEA or school.

Section Two: The emergence of special educational needs (1971–1989)

In the early 1970s teachers and parents requested a survey of the national provision for disadvantaged children. An investigation of the education of handicapped and backward pupils resulted in a survey of the whole field of provision in both mainstream and special schools; this was completed in 1978 under the chair of Mary Warnock. The aims of the report were summed up as follows (Warnock, 1982, p. 56):

> We wanted to very much get away from the statutory categories of handicap within the confines of which the provision of special education had been contained. We wanted to widen the scope of any new legislation there might be, so that it could cover not only provision for the 2% of children who, at the time we wrote, were being educated in special schools, but for something more like the 20% of all children at school.

Many of the report's recommendations were premised on epidemiological research which suggested that 1 in 5 children had special educational needs (Croll and Moses, 1985). The Warnock Committee considered that they had not found anything new but were merely commenting on good practice in schools. Five key recommendations were made in the report regarding the education of pupils with disability (Warnock, 1978, pp. 338–42):

- the 1944 Act's statutory categories should be removed and the concept of SEN widened

- children with SEN should have their needs assessed

- assessment procedures should involve five stages

- parental involvement in the assessment procedure should be encouraged

- there should be an expansion of LEA advisory and support services.

Significantly, the report's recommendations included the integration of pupils with SEN into mainstream education. However, the level of integration indicated in the report was a limited form of education provision for pupils with SEN; limited in that pupils, although physically located in a mainstream setting, would have to adapt in order to fit the location and culture of established forms of teaching and learning. That is to say the pupil, as opposed to the school system, was required to change and if unable to do so the placement would be deemed a failure. Examples of integration are providing pupils with disability half days in, or limited social experiences of, the mainstream school. The stigma of failure if an integrated placement was not successful is therefore located with the pupil.

Significantly, preliminary findings of the Warnock Committee influenced the 1976 Education Act in promoting integration of pupils with SEN into mainstream schools and recommending the removal of all categories of handicap by replacing these with a broader concept of special educational needs. The 1976 Education Act encouraged integration according to the following criteria:

- that this was in accordance with parental wishes

- that the child's educational needs could be met

- that it was consistent with the efficient use of resources

- that it would not detract from the education of the rest of the class.

In 1980 the government produced a White Paper on Special Needs in Education, which established Special Educational Needs (SEN) as a legal term referring to pupils with learning difficulties and/or disabilities. The paper was focused on economic interests and did not directly advocate the integration of all pupils with SEN into mainstream schools; however, by including the Warnock Report's recommendations, it opened the door for the integrationist movement. The 1981 Education Act acknowledged that the education of a child deemed having a special need should take place where and when appropriate within the mainstream setting. Furthermore it advocated that all statutory categories of handicap be removed and in their place practitioners make use of the term Special Educational Needs (SEN). Much confusion surrounded the concept of SEN but the 1981 Act gave a clear and precise account of what SEN meant (DES, 1981):

A child has special educational needs if he has a learning difficulty, which calls for special provision to be made for him.

The immediate effect of the 1978 Warnock Report and the subsequent 1981 Education Act was the development of long-awaited LEA policies on integration. The 1981 Education Act established a statementing procedure whereby children deemed to have special needs within the mainstream sector were entitled to further funding to meet their needs. Statements were to be issued to children deemed having the most serious needs in a mainstream school; others with needs were to be catered for within the school's overall budget. Statements would ensure that pupils would be delegated extra funding from their LEA (Pike, 1996).

Seven years on, the 1988 Education Reform Act (ERA) introduced a policy that was to place SEN provision within the context of parental choice, devolved funding and a national curriculum for all pupils. Norwich (1993, p. 79) commented:

> *The integrative movement was central to the Warnock philosophy and was based on the underlying principle that the aims of education were the same for all children. The significance of the 1988 National Curriculum needs to be understood in this context.*

The National Curriculum promoted the integration of pupils with SEN to mainstream settings. The ERA advocated that pupils with SEN should be treated equally to those without SEN in terms of access to mainstream education. This policy was expressed through pupil entitlement to a common curriculum.

KEY QUESTIONS

- How have government policies and reports shaped and informed SEN practice since 1870?

- Did the establishment of a separate education system for pupils with disabilities in the nineteenth century bring about significant gains for educational theory and practice?

- Did the ideas within the Warnock Report, included in the 1981 and 1988 Education Acts, bring about significant positive change with regards to how children with disability were educated?

- Was the change in language use and the promotion of 'integration' in the late 1970s and 1980s effective in establishing an equitable education system?

- What can managers and practitioners gain from the experiences of educationalists since 1870?

The integration of pupils with SEN into mainstream education focused attention once again on how such pupils were labelled. Several researchers (Stakes and Hornby, 1997; Oliver, 1998), argued that the term Special Educational Needs emerged as part of the Politically Correct (PC) agenda instigated by disability rights groups in the 1960s. Implicit in Corbett's (1994, p. 17) definition of political correctness is a link between the use of language and attitude towards others; political correctness is:

> *... about paying careful attention to the language we habitually use. It is particularly concerned with ... sensitivity to the ways in which people prefer themselves to be described and defined.*

The agenda of disability rights groups illustrated by the Union of the Physically Impaired Against Segregation (UPIAS), which was established in 1974, was to challenge society's perception. Oliver (1998, p. 88) later commented that:

> *From the mid 1970s onwards, organisations controlled and run by disabled people such as UPIAS, the Liberation Network, and the early disabled women's movement in the form of Sisters Against Disability (SAD), all shared the same basic goals: namely to secure equal rights for disabled people and to remove negative discrimination in all its forms. Similar goals were later adopted by the British Council of Disabled People (BCODP).*

Advocates of the new system believed that the use of SEN as a collective term would enable all children to be perceived as equals and worthy of a fair and equitable education regardless of disability (Barton and Tomlinson, 1984). Norwich (1996, p. 100) stated:

> *The SEN concept is associated with placing everyone along a continuum, based on the assumption that there is no clear and categoric distinction between the handicapped and the non-handicapped.*

Although significant, the PC agenda in the education of children with SEN can be a concern especially for practitioners in the field. Corbett (1994, p. 17) suggested that:

> *... an excessive vigilance to every nuance of vocabulary, every element of body language and all careless behaviours can make us so uneasy that we fear to speak or act spontaneously.*

As practitioners and managers, it is important to challenge consistently bias in language, particularly that which may lead to bias in practice. However, it is more than mere language that needs addressing if the reality of one's practice is to be inclusive. To be productive in pedagogy, practitioners need to be aware of issues of social justice and equity (Allan, 2003).

Activity 1.1 provides a prompt for practitioners and managers when determining individual and team views and use of language associated with special educational needs and inclusion.

**ACTIVITY 1.1: CONNECTING PRACTITIONER
THOUGHT, COMMUNICATION AND ACTION**

In line with the importance of language use, the following series of questions should be used to develop reflective practice through **thought** to **communication** to **action** so that awareness of practice becomes clearer and connections to attitudes apparent. This growth in self-awareness is imperative to develop reflective practice in accordance with inclusive aims.

- What do I understand by the label 'Special Educational Needs'?

- What does 'Inclusion' mean to me?

- How do I support all my learners?

- How do I refer to my learners?

- Is my pedagogy productive to all my learners?

- Is my classroom a just classroom?

Executive summary

- Inclusive schooling implies providing all children, regardless of race, language, disability, class and geographical location, with equitable and effective education.

- Inclusive schooling demands that practitioners, researchers and academics engage with their thinking and perceptions of what constitutes effective education for ALL children.

- The 1921 Education Act instituted five categories for those children deemed to have a handicap and therefore to be defective or unable to access a mainstream education.

- The medical model of disability promotes a deficit view of the learner and external factors are not considered causal.

- The 1944 Education Act established ten categories for those children deemed to have a handicap.

- During the 1960s a wave of disability rights groups emerged and built on this materialist discourse. They argued that effective educational provision for children with disabilities could and should be found within the mainstream.

- The 1970 Education Act integrated those formerly referred to as 'imbeciles' in the 1921 Education Act into the special education setting.

- The 1978 Warnock Report promoted integration and suggested the ten categories used for pupils with disabilities be replaced by a spectrum of SEN.

- The 1981 Education Act acknowledged that, where and when appropriate, the education of a child deemed having a special need should take place within the mainstream setting.

■ The 1988 Education Act advocated that pupils with SEN be treated equally in that they are given access to mainstream education. These values were expressed in the principle of a common curriculum for all pupils.

■ Exploring practitioner thoughts, communication and action helps to illuminate values and attitudes.

Further reading

Sandow, S. (ed.) (1994), *Whose Special Need?* London: Paul Chapman Publishing
Schonell, F. (1924), *Backwardness in the Basic Subjects*, London: Oliver and Boyd
Tomlinson, S. (1982), *A Sociology of Special Education*, London: Routledge and Keegan Paul

Devolution and Inclusion

CHAPTER 2: KEY QUESTIONS TO BE CONSIDERED
■ What is inclusion?
■ How and why has this ideology influenced education practice since the early 1990s?
■ What is inclusion in practice?
■ What have been the experiences of parents, pupils, managers and practitioners regarding the implementation of inclusive school policies since 1993?
■ How have primary and secondary practitioners implemented inclusive practice?
■ What practices enable the practitioner to think, understand, communicate and operate in a positive inclusive way at the same time raising the learning outcomes of their learners?

Introduction

This chapter provides an overview of government policies since 1993 that have impacted on the management of teaching and learning in mainstream primary and secondary schools. This chapter aims to enable practitioners and managers to further develop their understanding of inclusion, how it has emerged and how the practitioner has a fundamental role in its understanding and practice within the school community. The critical questioning of government policy will focus on raising academic standards while achieving diversity in the classroom through inclusive teaching and learning. Definitions of inclusion and SEN are given in the context of contemporary research into the opinions, attitudes and experiences of practitioners, parents and pupils. The chapter is presented in four sections:

■ Section One: Defining inclusion, government policy and emerging tensions

■ Section Two: The pupils' voice

■ Section Three: The parents'/guardians' voice

■ Section Four: The teachers' voice

Section One: Defining inclusion, government policy and emerging tensions

In 1994, the introduction of the Code of Practice resulted in confusion within schools and LEAs over how best to make arrangement for all pupils to access the National Curriculum and how to identify and provide statements for additional funding. The Department for Education (DfE) attempted to devise coherent and specific guides for mainstream schools for the provision for pupils with SEN. The guides were finally produced as circulars and sent to schools in 1994 as detailed below:

Department for Education Circulars 1994

Circular number	Circular name
2/94	Local Management of Schools.
3/94	The Development of Special Schools.
6/94	The Organisation of Special Educational Provision.
8/94	Pupil Behaviour and Discipline.
9/94	The Education of Children with Emotional and Behavioural Difficulties.
10/94	Exclusions from School.
11/94	The Education by LEAs of Children Otherwise than at School.
12/94	The Education of Sick Children (published jointly with the Department of Health).
13/94	The Education of Children being looked after by Local Authorities (published jointly with the Department of Health).

The authors consider that inclusion acknowledges the impact of the social environment upon pupils' abilities to learn and develop. Inclusion seeks to facilitate diversity and to ensure pupils' needs are viewed equitably and met fairly (Ainscow, 1995, 1999; Thomas et al., 1998). These values are evident in recent academic thinking and government policy relating to mainstream primary and secondary education. This view of inclusion stems from the social model of disability described by Barnes (1996, p. 1):

> *Disability is a complex form of social oppression or institutionalised discrimination ... theoretical analysis has shifted from individuals and their impairment to disabling environments and hostile attitudes.*

The social model of disability and related notions of inclusion emphasise that response to individual need is the responsibility of the primary or secondary school community i.e. the school adapting its environment and policy to fit the pupil's needs. Allan (2000, p. 1) explained:

> *Inclusive education is ... an approach which requires both increasing participation and the removal of barriers to radical school reform.*

It is important to understand the difference between practices of integration and inclusion. This understanding will help practitioners to develop insight into the values that inform practice. Chapter 1 has placed inclusion in its historical context, linking it to the human rights and social justice agendas of the disability rights movement (Barnes, 1996; Oliver, 1998). This movement led to increased integration in education supported by social policy and funding.

Following the 1988 Education Reform Act, legislation and practice was influenced by the advice and recommendations of the 1989 United Nations Rights of the Child and subsequently the 1994 United Nations Educational, Scientific and Cultural Organisation. (UNESCO) Salamanca Statement. These papers encouraged the educational and social inclusion of children and adults with SEN. Table 2.1 summarises the aims and objectives of the 1994 UNESCO Salamanca Statement.

Table 2.1 The UNESCO Salamanca Statement on Special Educational Needs

1. Every child has a fundamental right to education and must be given the opportunity to achieve and maintain an acceptable level of learning.

2. Every child has unique characteristics, interests, abilities and learning needs.

3. Educational systems should be designed and educational programmes implemented to take account of the wide diversity of these characteristics.

4. Those with special educational needs must have access to regular schools, which should accommodate them within a child-centred pedagogy capable of meeting their needs.

5. Regular schools with this inclusive orientation are the most effective means of combating discriminatory attitudes, creating welcoming communities, building an inclusive society and achieving education for the majority of children, and improving the efficiency and ultimately the effectiveness of the entire system.

During this period there was a distinct move by practitioners away from the view that the best place for pupils with SEN was in a segregated environment. Croll and Moses (2003) followed-up a previous study of 1998, which compared primary school teacher attitudes towards SEN, how teachers defined SEN and subsequent levels of SEN in classrooms with an earlier study in 1981; both projects took place in the same primary schools. Croll and Moses detected a significant change in teachers' attitudes towards pupils with SEN, with practitioners reporting more positive conditions and practices towards all pupil learning. In practice, the number of pupils with SEN in their classrooms had increased, from 18.8% of pupils in 1981 to 26.1% in 1998. While this change is significant, Table 2.2 lists the variables that impacted on this outcome other than a trend of moving pupils from special school to mainstream education.

Table 2.2 Variables contributing to increases in pupils with SEN in mainstream education

- Development in teacher professional knowledge of SEN through Initial Teacher Education, Continuing Professional Development (CDP) and In-Service Education and Training (INSET)

- Changes in teacher perceptions

- Changes in pedagogy and learning

- Changes to curriculum

- Real changes in the educational needs of children

- Changes in identifying children with SEN

- Changes in school and local authority management structures as instigated in the 1988 Reform Act: Local Management of Schools (LMS)

- Increased involvement of external agencies in the school environment

- Successful placement of pupils in the mainstream as opposed to special school sector

- Funding issues relating to the identification of pupils with SEN.

The 1993 Education Act promoted the education of all pupils in mainstream schools. It led to the Code of Practice (CoP) (DfE, 1994a), which gave schools further guidance and promoted the use of Individual Education Plans (IEPs) in managing the learning of pupils with SEN. Following the CoP, practitioners requested more prescriptive guidance regarding how to assess and educate increasing numbers of pupils with SEN in their classrooms (Norwich, 1997; Mittler, 2000; Croll and Moses, 2003). Although initially welcomed, there were underlying tensions and expressions of concern that the CoP would lead to an inordinate amount of bureaucracy and work for schools. Thompson (1997, p. 2), then Head of the Policy Unit for the Association of Teachers and Lecturers (ATL), commented:

> *The introduction of the SEN CoP has led to the evolution of a job unique in schools, that of the Special Educational Needs Co-ordinator. The implications of the SEN CoP and the SENCO role were not adequately thought through before the imposition of the Code ... There seems to be a danger in these standards that there is ..., 'pressure' but without support.*

The CoP's main emphasis was on integration and had been intended to empower schools to manage the needs of pupils with SEN. The key member of staff responsible for its analysis and implementation was identified as the Special Educational Needs Co-ordinator (SENCO), a new managerial position for primary and secondary schools. In many schools the SENCO role replaced the member of staff responsible for 'special' education. Table 2.3 depicts key recommendations regarding the role of the SENCO.

Table 2.3 The SENCO's statutory and recommended responsibilities (DfE, 1994a, p. 9)

- The day-to-day operation of the school's SEN policy

- Liaising with and advising fellow teachers

- Co-ordinating provision for children with SEN

- Maintaining the school's SEN register and overseeing the records on all pupils with SEN

- Liaising with parents of children with SEN

- Contributing to the in-service training of staff

- Liaising with external agencies including the educational psychology service and other support agencies, medical and social services and voluntary bodies.

The significance of the CoP was to enhance the role of the classroom teacher and middle/senior managers which in turn resulted in an increase to their workload (Lewis and Neill, 1996; Lewis et al., 1996; Thompson, 1997). Table 2.4 presents various research evidence regarding the unacceptable demands and impacts the CoP had upon primary and secondary professionals undertaking the role of SENCO.

Table 2.4 Research findings on the role of the SENCO, 1995–1999

Garner (1995, p. 7)	*The CoP fails to acknowledge important resource issues, notably that SENCOs will have far greater responsibility without being given adequate time to fulfil either the planning or the execution of their newly expanded set of duties.*
Dyson and Gains (1995, p. 55)	*The management structures which characterise most schools are hangovers from an earlier time when special needs was a largely separate area of activity … SENCOs who do not have access to the senior level of school management hierarchy are simply not in a position to carry out the requirements of their role.*
Garner (1996a, p. 186)	*SENCOs have to deal with important professional dilemmas. These include defining a new managerial role, their contribution to effective whole-school policy implementation and a paradoxical situation in which SENCOs have assumed more status in the eyes of colleagues but are under increasing stress because of the chronic lack of time available to them for Code-related administration.*

Lewis et al. (1997, p. 3–4)	*SENCOs welcomed the potential of the Code but were facing difficulties in implementing the recommendations … The main obstacles to implementing the Code were lack of resources, time constraints and low status.*

For many primary schools, the deputy head teacher had taken on the role of SENCO in 1994, but in secondary it had remained predominately the domain of middle managers (Gibson, 1999; Blandford and Gibson, 2000). The fact that changes to SEN practice would impact on all phases and disciplines in schools was disregarded. Given the conflict over policy and teacher workload, in conjunction with the Disability Rights Commission (DRC), the Department for Education and Employment (DfEE) amended the Code of Practice. Further amendments were made to Section Four of the 1995 Disability Discrimination Act which resulted in the Special Educational Needs and Disability Act (SENDA) (DfES, 2001a). The revised Code of Practice focused on managing increased demands upon the school community as well as making best use of resources and managing the role of SENCO within the school's senior management structure. Furthermore it reflected the increasing recognition of social rights issues and equal opportunities demonstrated by impact of parental choice, LEA accountability and the Office for Standards in Education (OfSTED) on mainstream education.

In 1997, the Labour government brought a change in policy development and a stronger commitment to inclusive education in particular for inclusive schooling and the establishment of inclusive classrooms (Tilstone et al., 1998; Mittler, 2000; Blandford and Gibson, 2001). This policy was presented in the Green Paper (DfEE, 1997) and the Programme of Action (DfEE, 1998) clearly indicating that the government was committed to increasing the diversity of learners in the mainstream setting. Government was also committed to raising academic standards in mainstream settings. Conflict emerged between these two policy drives: the former promoting inclusion and the belief that children who learn together regardless of special needs or disabilities will invariably be able to live together; the latter promoting increased competition leading to marketisation of education within local school communities. This conflict is explained by Mittler (2000, p. 104):

> *The publication of national test results in league tables is obviously part of the political objective of enforcing accountability. Although the league tables now contain additional information, the information reported fails to do justice to the work of schools in teaching 'the whole curriculum', nor can such tables reflect the values and ethos of a school.*

Inclusion

It is necessary to understand the meaning and aims of inclusion within the current context, while allowing for an appreciation of inclusive values and their impact on pupil learning. The Centre for Studies on Inclusive Education (CSIE) (2000, p. 1) explains what inclusion in education involves:

- Valuing all students and staff equally.

- Increasing the participation of students in, and reducing their exclusion from, the cultures, curricula and communities of local schools.

- Restructuring the cultures, policies and practices in schools so that they respond to the diversity of students in the locality.

- Reducing barriers to learning and participation for all students, not only those with impairments or those who are categorised as 'having special educational needs'.

- Learning from attempts to overcome barriers to the access and participation of particular students to make changes for the benefit of students more widely.

- Viewing the difference between students as resources to support learning, rather than as problems to be overcome.

- Acknowledging the right of students to an education in their locality.

- Improving schools for staff as well as for students.

- Emphasising the role of schools in building community and developing values, as well as in increasing achievement.

- Fostering mutually sustaining relationships between schools and communities.

- Recognising that inclusion in education is one aspect of inclusion in society.

In response to professionals' requests for more explicit guidance on establishing and evaluating their inclusive school communities, a toolkit was published (DfES, 2001c). The toolkit provides suggestions and practical advice on how to implement the CoP in response to practitioner needs and the school community. Subsequent to these revisions the Department for Education and Science (DfES) published further supporting guidance, *Data Collection by Type of Special Educational Needs* (DfES, 2003), which emerged as part of government's Pupil Level Annual Schools Census (PLASC). It provides detailed guidance on categories of SEN. The government believed that these categories would enable the DfES to study trends and monitor the outcomes of initiatives and interventions on pupils with different types of SEN. Table 2.5 details the categories.

One consequence of the revised CoP has been good practice in mainstream primary and secondary schools with the identification of a team responsible for meeting the needs of learners with SEN and establishing an inclusive school culture. Subsequently, the team has a responsibility with school leaders to scrutinise school aims and practices. Furthermore the team concerns itself with members' beliefs, understandings and professional development in the field of inclusive education. The team contains representatives from the school's SEN department, either SENCO or deputy SENCO, a sample of school teachers (faculty based or key stage based depending on primary or secondary setting), Teaching Assistants (TAs), the governing body and when possible parents and pupils, the aims of these teams being to strengthen understanding and subsequently practices of inclusive education in their school communities.

Table 2.5 Collecting information about types of Special Educational Need (DfES, 2003, p. 1)

Category	Areas of need
A	**Cognition and learning needs** ■ Specific Learning Difficulty ■ Moderate Learning Difficulty ■ Severe Learning Difficulty ■ Profound and Multiple Learning Difficulty
B	**Behavioural, Emotional and Social Developmental Needs** ■ Behaviour, Emotional and Social Difficulty
C	**Communication and Interaction Needs** ■ Speech, Language and Communication Needs ■ Autistic Spectrum Disorder
D	**Sensory and/or Physicial Needs** ■ Visual Impairment ■ Hearing Impairment ■ Multi-sensory Impairment ■ Physical Disability
OTH	**Other**

Schools were advised to share the roles and responsibilities of the SENCO and make more efficient use of external resources provided by the LEA as well as working in partnership with parents and pupils to revise the five-stage process leading to a statement of additional funding to a three-stage process. The following summarises the roles and responsibilities of the whole-school community (DfES, 2001a, 1: 31):

> *Provision for pupils with special educational needs is a matter for the school as a whole. In addition to the governing body, the school's head teacher, the SENCO or SEN team and all other members of staff have important responsibilities. In practice the division of the day-to-day responsibilities is a matter for individual schools, to be decided in light of a school's circumstances and size, priorities and ethos.*

The role of the practitioner is fundamental to fostering understanding of inclusive thinking and practice in the school community. In doing so, it is necessary that the practitioner has an understanding regarding the opinions, attitudes and experiences of colleagues, parents and pupils. Allan (2003, p. 178) argues:

> *Becoming Inclusive … means becoming political; listening to what children and their parents say about what inclusion means to them; and recognising the way in which we ourselves are implicated in practices that exclude.*

The following definition of SEN (DfES, 2001a, 1:3) is current policy which impacts on the practitioner's and manager's understanding and practice:

Children have special educational needs if they have a learning difficulty, which calls for special educational provision to be made for them. Children have a learning difficulty if they:

a) have a significantly greater difficulty in learning than the majority of children of the same age; or

b) have a disability which prevents or hinders them from making use of educational facilities of a kind generally provided for children of the same age in schools within the area of the local education authority

c) are under compulsory school age and fall within the definition of (a) or (b) above and would do so if special educational provision was not made for them.

Children must not be regarded as having a learning difficulty solely because the language or form of language of their home is different from the language in which they will be taught. Special Educational provision means:

a) for children of two or over, educational provision which is additional to, or otherwise different from, the educational provision made generally for children of their age in schools maintained by the LEA, other than special schools in the same area

b) for children under two, educational provision of any kind.

Section Two: The pupils' voice

Recent key documents, *Every Child Matters: Next Steps* (DfES, 2004b) and the *Children's Charter* (Scottish Executive, 2004), are preparing the way for future practice in mainstream schools. As centres of collegiate, multi-agency practice, schools will be managing the interface between health, support and educational agencies. The importance of the individual within this setting cannot be overstated.

Much can be gained from the review of past policies and practices. As shown in Chapter 1 and the preceding section, there have been many policies to tackle the complexities of inclusion and the management of special educational needs. It is the authors' view that these inform current practice. What has been missing in the past is recognition of voice, the individual within the policy.

Practitioners in school play the role of *loco parentis*. They are not there solely to bestow knowledge on pupils, they are also there to assist in their pupils' fuller development as social beings and to work as part of a team in the construction of an effective and inclusive school community. It is important that teachers listen to the voices of pupils. The revised CoP (DfES, 2001a) comments on the importance of pupil participation in the assessment of learning needs, the compilation and subsequent evaluation of IEPs. Specifically, the government (DfES, 2001a, p. 27) states:

Children and young people with special educational needs have a unique knowledge of their own needs ... and views about what sort of help they would like ... They should, where possible, participate in all the decision-making processes that occur in education including the setting of learning targets and contributing to IEPs ...

This is a view held by the theorists Lewis and Lindsay (2000) and Roberts (2000), who comment on the importance of hearing the pupils' voice and providing room for practitioners to develop a perspective on the pupils' world. Roberts (2000, p. 238) explains:

It is clear that listening to children, hearing children and acting on what children say are three very different activities, although they are frequently elided as if they were not.

Shevlin and O'Moore (2000, p. 206) comment on the importance of hearing and acting on the disabled pupils' voice in education:

Young people with severe/profound intellectual disabilities are often excluded from meaningful participation in mainstream education. As a result they rarely have an opportunity to interact with their non-disabled peers ... and remain an isolated and marginalized group.

Learning together would appear to be a positive social and cognitive experience for pupils, having a long-term beneficial effect on the development and sustenance of relationship between the pupil with SEN and other pupils. How does inclusion impact on those pupils without SEN? Shevlin and O'Moore (2000) suggest that regular contact with those labelled as having SEN leads to more social acceptance and positive results in establishing and maintaining relationships. Learning in an inclusive classroom enables pupils to develop and build on their empathetic, communication and social awareness skills (Lewis, 1995b; Shevlin and O'Moore, 2000). Further, inclusion does not appear to have a negative impact on their cognitive development (Staub and Peck, 1994; Brownlee and Carrington, 2000). Lipsky and Gartner (1996, p. 15) claim that:

For non-disabled students, the near unanimous reports from teachers, parents and the students themselves are positive in terms of social behavioural outcomes, frequent reports of positive academic outcomes and no reports of negative effects academically.

Table 2.6 summarises research evidence that places pupils with SEN in the context of inclusive schooling.

Table 2.6 SEN research

Reference	Research findings
Baker et al. (1995, p. 152)	*The findings from three meta-analyses concerning the most effective setting for the education of students with disabilities reports ... that special needs students educated in regular classes do better academically and socially than comparable students in non-inclusive settings.*
Lipsky and Gartner (1996, p. 15)	*In general the 1994 and 1995 national studies (of inclusion) as well as other evaluation studies ... report positive student academic, behavioural and social outcomes for students with disabilities.*
Peetsma et al. (2001, p. 134)	*Studies of regular and special education as a whole demonstrate that pupils in special education perform less well on cognitive tasks and function less well psychosocially.*

While undertaking research into pupils' experiences of inclusion in schools, Norwich and Kelly (2004, p. 62) discovered that the majority of pupils with Moderate Learning Difficulties (MLD) preferred their learning and social experiences in a mainstream school. However, a high proportion of these pupils prefer learning support in withdrawal settings as either their main form of support or mixed with some in-class support. Although this advocates a move towards including pupils from special schools, it also suggests a preference for separate learning support alongside in-class support. It is therefore important to note the difference between an inclusive school and an inclusive classroom; the latter being addressed in Chapter 4. Table 2.7 summarises research findings by Peck et al. (1990, p. 244) that non-disabled adolescents perceive benefit from social relationships with peers who have disability.

Table 2.7 Six 'benefits' of association with peers who have disability

1. improved self-concept
2. social-cognitive growth
3. reduced fear of human differences
4. increased tolerance of other people
5. development of principles of personal conduct
6. relaxed and accepting friendships.

Section Three: The parents'/guardians' voice

Current government policy and educational literature emphasise the importance of schools establishing and maintaining relationships with parents. With regard to those pupils with SEN, it is fundamental to evaluate their needs effectively and subsequently evaluate the learning support provided that the school liaises with the pupil's parents. The revised CoP (DfES, 2001a) makes clear that accessing and working with parents or, in the case of 'looked after children', guardians is fundamental. The CoP (DfES, 2001a, p. 16) explains:

> *Partnership with parents plays a key role in promoting a culture of co-operation between parents, schools, LEAs and others. This is important in enabling children and young people with SEN to achieve their potential.*

Table 2.8 summarises research findings on the importance of hearing the parents' voice. The revised CoP (DfES, 2001a, 2: 7) outlines what inclusive schools should be endeavouring to achieve in accessing the parents' voice.

Table 2.8 The importance of the parents' voice

Reference	Research findings
Solity (1992, p. 120)	*Parents are increasingly seen as consumers within the education system and so it is important that parents and teachers establish an effective rapport with each other.*
Hornby (1995, pp. 20–21)	*A partnership model: teachers are viewed as being experts on education and parents are viewed as being experts on their children.*
Kelley-Laine (1998, p. 345)	*High achieving well-ordered schools are characterised by good home–school relationship.*
Kenworthy and Whittaker (2000, pp. 221–223)	*Ending the segregation of children depends on achieving a consensus, shared conviction between young people, parents, survivors of segregation, educationalists and policy makers.*
Mittler (2000, p. 151)	*Parents of children with exceptional needs have a particularly great need for working relationships with teachers based on understanding and trust.*

To make communication effective professionals should:

- Acknowledge and draw on parental knowledge and expertise in relation to their child
- Focus on the children's strengths as well as areas of additional need
- Recognise the personal and emotional investment of parents and be aware of their feelings

- Ensure parents understand procedures, are aware of how to access support in preparing their contributions, and are given documents to be discussed well before meetings
- Respect the validity of differing perspectives and seek constructive ways of reconciling different viewpoints
- Respect the differing needs parents themselves may have, such as a disability, or communication and linguistic barriers
- Recognise the need for flexibility in the timing and structure of meetings

In considering how to achieve the above aims it is recommended that SENCOs work closely with their school's SEN team. The role and management of the SEN team will be addressed in greater detail in Chapters 4 and 5. Mittler (2000, p. 153) states:

Every school needs its own home–school policy to go beyond fine words and include concrete proposals for achieving better working relationships with its parents and the local community.

Table 2.9 suggests necessary roles and responsibilities of the 'inclusive' school towards parents. These suggestions are to enable those working in a school SEN team to establish effective inclusive practices in accessing parental voice and support.

Since the revised CoP (DfES, 2001a, 2: 16), parent partnership services are a mandatory aspect of LEA provision. LEAs must ensure they make this resource available to parents either directly from their own services or indirectly, i.e. buying in a service.

All LEAs must make arrangements for parent partnership services. It is essential that parents are aware of the parent partnership service so that they know where they can obtain the information and advice they need. LEAs must therefore inform parents, schools and others about the arrangements for the service and how they can access it.

Parent partnership services appear to be a positive advocate for parents; supporting, advising and working for them if they disagree with LEA tribunal decisions regarding their child's school placement and/or a school's decision on meeting their child's needs (Mittler, 2000; Frederickson and Cline, 2002; Gross, 2002). Further details are provided in Chapter 3.

Table 2.9 How to successfully access the parents' voice

Recommendations	Establishing and evaluating
To ensure the following is made available upon request and that parents are aware of their rights to this information.	▪ School's SEN policy ▪ Support available in school and LEA ▪ Procedures for acting on parental concerns ▪ How to complain if they are unhappy with school's arrangements ▪ LEA services ▪ Local and national organisations that may be able to offer further advice and information.
To ensure parents are made aware and involved from the start of a pupil's SEN identification.	SENCO or named representative from the SEN team to keep a file on parent and pupil's details, recording and tracking all communication and details regarding pupil's SEN identification and assessment.
Home–school contracts making clear the role(s) and responsibilities of the SEN team and parents.	SENCO and parents to discuss contracts as part of regular meetings to evaluate pupil's SEN and IEP.
To ensure parents are provided with regular feedback regarding their child's progress.	SENCO or named representative from the SEN team to ensure copies of all files relevant to pupil's SEN identification, and assessment (e.g. those compiled by classroom teacher and/or tutor, LEA and in some cases educational psychologist (EP)) are sent to parents.
To ensure that parents understand the processes their child is going through in order that their school meets their SEN effectively.	SENCO or named representative from the SEN team to make regular recorded contact with parents by either home visits or telephone calls. To liaise with the parents in a sensitive manner, enabling them to share if they are feeling intimidated, threatened or confused.
Where problems do occur with breakdown in communication, to make contact and work closely with LEA parent partnership service.	SENCO or named representative from the SEN team to be aware of parent partnership service in their LEA. To note named officer(s) and ensure that, if needed, regular and recorded communication takes place.

Section Four: The teachers' voice

As educators, teachers and managers need to be aware of the school community in their practice. What are its values? What are current tensions? What do practitioners hope to achieve for pupils in their care? How can we do it in an inclusive way, i.e. working both in and with our community? In order to answer these questions practitioners must locate themselves as individuals within the community, becoming aware of their specific roles in helping the community to function inclusively and successfully (Baker et al., 1995; Reynolds, 1995).

How do practitioners fit into the government's current inclusive education plan and how do they ensure that they are the architects rather than the mere recipients of any new plans? Literature into attitude and impact of attitude upon practice suggests professionals who received effective provision in Initial Teacher Education (ITE) and Continuing Professional Development (CPD) hold positive attitudes towards and record positive experiences of, inclusion (Mittler, 1993; Avramedis et al., 2000; Marshall et al., 2002). Table 2.10 provides a summary of research into teachers' attitudes towards, and experiences of, inclusion.

Table 2.10 Teacher attitudes and experiences of inclusion

Reference	Research findings
Sebba and Sachdev (1997, p. 61)	*The experience of inclusive education appears to have a positive effect on teacher, pupil and parent attitudes, shifting attention away from the child's perceived disability on to the child as a person.*
Blandford and Gibson (2000 p. 6)	*In theory inclusion means ensuring all children have access to the mainstream … in practice it means a whole lot of difficulties especially for me.*
Marshall et al. (2002, p. 13)	*I'd feel positively challenged BUT would need more information to know the history of the child, the nature and cause of the disability, special training and more resources.*
Croll and Moses, (2003, p. 744)	*For the overwhelming majority of children with SEN in mainstream schools, the teacher felt that the regular classroom was the right place for the child. In nine out of ten cases the teacher said that the child should be in the regular classroom.*

As shown in preceding sections, teacher attitudes towards inclusion have become more positive and progressive since 1993; however, their experiences continue to highlight perceived need for more support and resources. Most ITE programmes provide training in SEN during the student teacher's school placement, i.e. via contact and interaction with the school's SENCO, TAs, trainee's mentor, and also by differentiating lesson plans in accordance with the needs of all their learners as an integral aspect of all ITE programmes (Mittler, 2000). Yet research suggests most Newly Qualified Teachers (NQTs) feel unprepared to meet the needs of their learners with SEN (Marshall et al., 2002). This perceived view might stem from beliefs and attitudes reflective of a medical model in that there is need for specialist teaching and resources to meet the types of educational needs of some pupils with SEN.

In attempting to build a positive attitude and experience of inclusive education, which challenges the attitude that Special Educational Needs is 'Not in my Subject Area' (Garner, 2000a), school communities need to allow space and time for teachers to share views, feelings and experiences. This should take place in an open and supportive climate as the importance and benefits of colleague interaction, support and peer review cannot be overstated. Specifically, teachers should be given time and space to collaborate in developing collective attitudes towards all learners. Such informal, reflective meetings would allow teachers to:

- share tips and insights, thus benefiting each other and, in so doing, building an inclusive school culture

- feel secure enough to respond and work with questions being asked of their practices, beliefs, understandings and professional knowledge.

The school's culture will have a significant impact on such practices. Chapter 3 shows how a school community can promote the values of a learning organisation where all members are willing and able to admit their shortcomings as well as ask each other for assistance and learn from each other's strengths, thus creating an inclusive and effective school community (Ainscow, 2001).

Practitioners also need to interact with colleagues in a supportive way when addressing issues of language, attitudes and practices that can inhibit the development of an inclusive school community. Many people with disabilities maintain that one of the most challenging barriers to their inclusion in society is that of negative language and attitudes held by those without disabilities. In the school community, it is important that practitioners are given the opportunity to explore their individual opinions and beliefs regarding disability. Brownlee and Carrington (2000, p. 100) maintain that:

> ... *structured opportunities to reflect on and question society's beliefs would allow ... teachers the opportunity to examine personal beliefs in relation to people who have a disability. Changes in beliefs and attitudes will only take place if the individual is challenged to see the inadequacy of his or her beliefs.*

ACTIVITY 2.1: STEPS TO WORKING TOWARDS INCLUSIVE PRACTICE

The following activity provides suggestions for practitioners who currently find the process of inclusion and the prospect of a changing school culture daunting.

- Get to know your school SENCO and/or school SEN team.

- Access the school's current SEN policy in order to familiarise yourself with the school's aims towards meeting the needs of all its learners.

- Read the DfES Programme of Action in order to familiarise yourself with current government policy aims and objectives. ▶

- Get a personal copy of the Code of Practice.

- Try to keep abreast of current developments in your LEA (SEN training sessions, INSET and/or CPD programmes). Information can be accessed direct from your LEA's web-site and via contacting the LEA officer with responsibility for SEN.

- Challenge the assumption that teaching pupils with SEN requires a certain type of specialist pedagogy. The National Association for Special Educational Needs suggests that effective use of available resources, e.g. TAs, pupils' views, professional abilities and differentiation in collaboration with colleagues, is good practice for all pupils including those with SEN.

- If you still feel unable to meet the needs of a learner then contact your SENCO. They will assist and take on any necessary further assessment of the learner.

- Do not attempt to diagnose a learner's SEN. There are currently so many labels that any practitioner, whether newly qualified or well experienced, may get confused. Leave it to a specialist who can be accessed by the SENCO.

- If you are keen to be proactive in the development of your inclusive school, offer your support on the school's SEN team, or if there is not one then suggest to the SENCO that a team be established.

- Finally know your own limits and ask for help if you need it. Working as part of a growing inclusive school culture will demand openness and community spirit.

This page can be photocopied. © *Managing Special Educational Needs*, Gibson and Blandford, 2005

A school community that works together with common dialogue and understanding can establish an effective and inclusive school (see Chapter 3). The adage of 'no man is an island' holds true; people need people and relationship. Humans are inherently social beings, learning through, with and from others (Wright, 1971). The resulting diversity and conflict which this brings is a necessary part of living; furthermore it is a necessary part of a school community's inclusive progress. To summarise, practitioners need to be enabled to ask, to discuss and be active contributors to their school's vision and subsequent practise of inclusion. Table 2.11 summarises the importance of dialogue in the establishment of an inclusive school community, where the voices of pupils, parents and teachers are respected and listened to.

The practices advocated in this section suggest a move towards more collegiate leadership. A collegiate school culture in many ways reflects the values of inclusion, i.e. where all voices are heard and acted on. Thus if effective inclusive school communities are to develop, the traditional hierarchical approach to school leadership and management needs to be challenged and revised (Gibson, 1999; Ainscow, 2001). Leadership needs to be shared, voices from all levels and parts of the school community listened to and representatives need to work together towards their common aim for inclusion (see Chapters 3 and 4).

Table 2.11 The importance of dialogue: one, other, our

To feel respected 'one' needs to be heard.

To respect the 'other' 'one' needs to listen.

To establish a learning community with shared values and aims 'one' needs to work with the 'other'.

To establish 'our' common aims we need to work 'together';

To openly share 'our' fears and insecurities;

To openly share 'our' values and attitudes;

To openly share 'our' strengths and weaknesses;

To agree on communal goals and ways in which to achieve them;

To evaluate and revise 'our' practices regularly.

KEY QUESTIONS

■ How have government policies since 1993 shaped and informed SEN practice?

■ Did the ideas within the 1994 and subsequent 2001 CoP enable your school to progress towards inclusive practice?

■ Do you think language, attitudes, and practices have changed significantly in your school community since 1994?

Executive summary

■ Inclusion seeks to facilitate diversity, variety and to celebrate difference as a spectrum upon which all pupils are viewed equitably.

■ The social model of disability and notions of inclusion emphasise that inclusive practice is the responsibility of the primary or secondary school, i.e. the school must change its environment and policy to fit the pupil's needs.

■ The initial CoP enhanced the role of the classroom teacher and middle/senior managers as SENCO in assessing, providing for and evaluating the needs of learners with SEN.

■ The revised CoP suggested that the former roles and responsibilities of the SENCO be shared within a team representative of the school community.

■ Mainstream primary and secondary school will have a team responsible for meeting the needs of their learners with SEN and establishing an inclusive school culture.

■ Teachers need to listen to the voices, experiences and views of their pupils.

■ Schools need to listen to the voices, experiences and views of their parents.

 ■ Learning in an inclusive school is a positive social and cognitive experience for the pupil with disability.

■ Practitioners and managers need to feel secure enough to work in a learning environment where questions will be asked of their practices, beliefs, understandings and professional knowledge.

Further reading

Centre for Studies on Inclusive Education (CSIE) (2000), *Index for Inclusion: developing learning and participation in schools*. Bristol: CSIE
Lewis, A. (1995b), *Children's Understanding of Disability*, London: Routledge
Thomas, G. and Vaughan, M. (2004), *Inclusive Education*, Berkshire: Open University
Vincent, C. (2004), *Including Parents*, Berkshire: Open University

The School as a **3** Community

<table>
<tr><td colspan="2">CHAPTER 3: KEY QUESTIONS TO BE CONSIDERED</td></tr>
<tr><td>■</td><td>What is meant by community?</td></tr>
<tr><td>■</td><td>What is an effective school culture?</td></tr>
<tr><td>■</td><td>How do managers and practitioners determine ethos?</td></tr>
<tr><td>■</td><td>What is the impact of a pupil's home on school experiences?</td></tr>
<tr><td>■</td><td>What can be learnt from community and social initiatives practised elsewhere in education?</td></tr>
</table>

Introduction

If a school is to be inclusive, it will need to locate itself within society. Managers and practitioners will then need to consider their place within the broader context. This chapter defines schools as a community within a community. As such, schools reflect community needs, both social and educational. Essentially, schools exist to enable learning and teaching to take place, which does not happen in a vacuum. Relationships with parents and the broader community are central to the effectiveness of schools. The chapter will discuss issues based on research undertaken in a range of schools, nationally and internationally. The chapter also illustrates community partnerships in action through two case studies: the first, a family-based project that began in 1994 and is now established practice in different forms in a significant number of LEAs; while the second focuses on community music projects in England and Portugal. This chapter is presented in four sections:

■ Section One: How schools are a community within a community

■ Section Two: The relationship between school and the community

■ Section Three: The advantages of increased parental involvement in schools

■ Section Four: Two case studies focusing on the development of school-
                  and community-based educational and social initiatives.

Section One: Defining schools as a community

If schools are to be inclusive, every school should be central to its local community. Managers and practitioners have a responsibility to understand that their school has to become a community within a community. Members of the school will be members of their local community reflecting its beliefs and values, conveyed through the action, behaviour and attitudes of the pupils, teaching and non-teaching staff, parents, governors and LEA.

Community can be defined as multidimensional within:

- location – where it is, the influence of the environment and systems of control

- structure – the administrative elements and guidance that determine equality of provision

- process – the management of people and development of a shared understanding of beliefs and values.

All members of the school, including those with special educational needs, as participants in the school and local community, should be encouraged to have a shared commitment to the creation of the school community. It is axiomatic that schools need organisational structures, aims and guiding rules if they are to be effective (see Chapter 5). As active players in the daily life of the school, pupils, teachers, parents, governors and support agencies need to relate to each other, sharing an understanding of the goals and targets that are to be achieved in an effective school (see Chapter 5). The determination of these goals is:

- reflective, in that the school mirrors the local community, sharing key players and their beliefs and values

- individual, as all members will have their own identity with their personal goals and objectives

- collective, as shared understanding of common beliefs and values will create a sense of community bound together by a recognisable identity and geographical location.

Community

The principles on which community provision is built are based on certain assumptions that relate to inclusive practice:

- education is part of social provision, strongly related to all other branches of social provision; education does not exist just as an academic entity

- social provision is determined by the prevailing social and economic framework of society

- throughout civilised history, the level of social provision has sustained societies in an unequal manner, balancing those who 'have' with those who 'have not'

- both social and educational provision have become more centrally controlled

- there has been a move towards devolution of power at an operational level, reflecting the need to provide community-type activities led by the community

- there is a greater emphasis on participation that has contributed to the emancipation of the teacher.

Within the context of community, it is necessary to consider how education contributes to the life-long experience of its members, including those with special educational needs. The home, local area and neighbourhood all contribute to the educational experience of each pupil. As a consequence there are varying degrees of good and bad influences on members of the school community. There is a need for the education system to enter into dialogue with the local community and to recognise its impact on the school. The management of SEN in schools should reflect the factors that determine the nature and culture of the community. In sum:

- Special and cultural interaction: the school can exert its influence on the life and minds of the people. Equally the neighbourhood, home and culture of the people can influence the school. The totality of the experiences of all those concerned in the educational process have an effect upon each other.

- Administration and control: the geographical and managerial system within the social and cultural framework. The structure gives shape and form to the beliefs and values of the community in its social and cultural being.

Critically, education in schools should be concerned with education within and for communities, not of communities (Poster, 1982). Community education, as with all education, begins with and for the individual. The role of the community educator is not dissimilar to the traditional role of the teacher: to educate individuals in order that they become autonomous and are able to participate in the community in which they choose to live. The element of choice is important; some members of the community may wish to remain in the same setting for much of their lives while others may choose to experience other communities. Education should provide individuals with the tools whereby they are able to make such choices.

School culture

As schools function within a community there is a need to create an identity that acknowledges and reflects where the community is and where it would like to be; this is also applicable to pupils, parents, teachers and support agencies (see Chapter 6).

Schools, like other communities, have their own characteristics and personalities. An understanding of the culture of schools is required before considering the management of SEN. The culture of each school is determined by individual and collective beliefs and values. Schools do not consist of homogenous groups of people with shared identities; schools are collections of individuals within a shared culture. The vision for the school is contained in the school development plan and policy statements that provide the rationale for practice. A school culture will manifest itself in many forms:

- practice – rites, rituals and ceremonies

- communications – stories, legends, symbols and slogans

- physical forms – location, style and condition of the school buildings, fixtures and fittings

- common language – phrases or jargon common to the school.

Ethos

Differences between schools may be explained in terms of organisational and social structure which also reflect the interpersonal relationships that create the ethos, the shared beliefs and values. The whole-school feeling exists to such an extent that it drives the school as a community towards achieving goals. An intangible relationship between community and ethos exists but the link is difficult to define. Ethos is multidimensional, as no single definition would apply to the many situations that occur in the life of the school community. Managers and practitioners create school ethos through values and behaviours that reflect values portrayed in policies and practice.

Analysis of school management and community is often directed at the individual teacher, whose skills in managing young people are so consequential to the life of the classroom (Hargreaves, 1984). The general ethos, climate or philosophy of a school has its own powerful consequences. The teacher and the pupil are interdependent; what is unclear is precisely how this interaction works.

Environment

There is a distinctive link between the atmosphere created in schools and their environment. An uncared-for school building, regardless of age, will reflect an uncaring community. Working in an environment that is in need of repair (as most schools are) creates stress; working in an environment that is unhealthy is not conducive to effective teaching and learning. Members of the school community need encouragement in order to fulfil their potential; a stimulating environment will produce stimulating results. Members of the school community need to consider how to create a positive environment. This may include:

- good quality displays of pupils' work and achievements covering full range of ability

- bright, open spaces with carpeted floors and plants, pictures and photographs

- clean buildings: no litter, adequate bins that are emptied, working toilet facilities

- supervised areas for study

- adequate facilities for every subject, e.g. PE and music store areas.

The management of the school environment is the responsibility of everyone in the school community. The development and maintenance of the environment can be a key activity within the school and help with the inclusion of pupils with SEN. Much can be made of any school building. Community is an essential concern of schools; as such the development and maintenance of a sense of community is a primary function.

Section Two: School, home and the community

In his book, *Democracy and Education*, Dewey (1960) referred to the social function of education but called for the removal of boundaries imposed by the scholastic tradition of the Middle Ages to a broad and comprehensive approach based on relations between the individual and society, the individual and the environment, and the school and the community. Dewey warns against the separation of the school from the life of the community, arguing that the greatest waste in the school for the learner stems from her/his inability to apply the acquired experience learnt in the classroom to a use in everyday life.

Durkheim (1967) ascribes major importance to the social functions of education, defining it as the creation of a common denominator among humans, bestowing meaning on human actions and laying the foundations of social cohesion. In Durkheim's opinion, every individual has inseparable entities within; one of these is the individualist identity, comprising all the mental conditions that relate to ourselves and events in our personal life. The second is the social entity, consisting of opinions, feelings and customs that express the group or groups that humans form, belong to and nurture. According to Durkheim, the purpose of education is to create the social entity, i.e. the socialisation of the individual from the moment of birth.

Machter (2000) found that the connection between education and society goes back to ancient times. Plato was the first to discover the potential inherent in education for the improvement of society. In his great work, *The Republic*, Plato details the attributes of the ideal society. In his opinion, the improvement of education depends mainly on the enhancement of social conditions, and the improvement of social conditions may be accomplished by education.

School and community

It emerges that the connection between the school and the community is not static but develops on a continuum. The level at which the school reaches its community and vice versa is their level of community orientation. There are three possible patterns of connection between the school and the community as described in the educational literature:

1. *The closed door pattern*: the school deals with all the child's educational and social problems, and community involvement and intervention are minimal. With a closed system like the laws of nature (entropy), the energy of the system will deteriorate. Therefore, according to Friedman (1986), the closed door policy towards the community needs feedback. In Friedman's view a closed door policy will waste energy without the right guidance. In the absence of constant input

from the parents and the community, the school will be unaware of changes occurring in these systems, and hence will be unable to adapt itself and its curricula to these changes and will keep degenerating.

2. *The open door pattern*: the school and the parents operate as open systems, so that information flows freely in both directions. The school with an open door policy makes the parents partners to their child's educational process and strives to become an influential factor in the life of the community. A basic assumption of systems theory is that the open system is designed to process the inputs of its external environment, only to return the processed product to the environment for its use and benefit. The exchange of energy occurs in a cyclic nature. The final and improved product serves as a new source of energy passing from the environment to the system. In this way the deteriorating entropy process is stopped (Katz and Kahn, 1978). According to Friedman (1986), the school with an open door policy receives its pupils from the parents, teaches them and raises their level of education, in order to return them to their community. In their adult life they will produce a new generation of pupils, whose contribution to their children's education is expected to be greater than that of their parents' generation.

3. *The balanced pattern*: the school and the parents set the degree of closeness or distance between them, in order to achieve their educational and social goals to the optimal extent. When the distance is large, the school has to bridge the gap and reach out to the community; when the distance is small, the school has to close its gates somewhat.

KEY QUESTIONS
■ How would you describe your school community?
■ How does your school participate in the community in which it is located?
■ What are the values that underpin practice in your school?
■ Does your school have an open or closed door policy? Or both?

Section Three: Parents and families

Parents and schools need to do everything they can to help their children with special educational needs relate co-operatively to adults and other children. An active partnership between parents and schools offers great benefits. The interaction between home circumstances and school practices is complicated particularly when there are medical or social problems but is important if a parents' voice is to be encouraged. Schools should provide welcoming environments (see Chapter 2). Schools can use prospectuses and other communications to convey and reinforce the nature of parental responsibility and the notion of home–school partnership. Contact with parents should not be confined to parents' evenings; it should be an integral part of school life. It may be possible to bring together groups of parents to discuss problems in an atmosphere of mutual support.

Schools have found home–school contracts to be of significant benefit in involving parents constructively in considering education plans. Such contracts, which specify the expectations of pupils, parents and the school, have proved useful in setting out for parents their particular responsibilities in relation to their child, and in defining the school's role and policies. Such contracts are likely to work best if they offer the prospect of benefits.

Sometimes a pupil with SEN may be with a foster parent or residential social worker, or with another relative because of a court order. These carers also have a general responsibility to work with the school and pupil. Teachers and governors should be alert to the difficulties and pressures that can arise from unstable family relationships and the impact of unemployment, homelessness, family bereavement, racial tension and illness. Sometimes family breakdown may result in pupils having very disrupted lives and moving between different homes, or moving out of areas where they had established friendships. For some pupils, the school may be the only secure, stable environment they have.

It has been shown that when pupils have relationships outside the family in which they feel valued and respected, this helps to protect them against adversity within the family. Pupils may nonetheless feel inhibited about discussing changes in their lives such as family breakdown. Some children take primary responsibility for caring for parents who are sick or disabled. This may have an adverse effect on pupils' emotional and educational development. The school's processes for recording and identifying pupils with problems should be sensitive to possible links between behaviour and other experiences in a child's life. This may lead to the need to involve other agencies or support services in order to assist the pupil's development.

The benefits of parental involvement in the school

Parental involvement in the school enriches the pupils' world and extends their horizons because, when the parents take part in the educational process, the pupils are exposed to a variety of people who represent different worlds in terms of life experience, age, occupation, hobbies and mentality; these encounters afford many opportunities for learning, enrichment and identification (Noy, 1984). Parental involvement serves as a personal example for each pupil and increases awareness of the importance of the community action (Stein and Harpaz, 1995). The benefit of parental involvement is also manifested in the pupil's personality and behavioural variables, such as improvement in self-image and learning habits, reduction in disciplinary problems and absenteeism, and rise in motivation – all particularly relevant to pupils with SEN (Raywid, 1984).

Parents benefit personally from their involvement, which enables them to deepen their knowledge of their child's world, the subjects taught, the teaching methods and effective forms of negotiation with children. The involvement allows the parents to share knowledge about their child with the staff and the teachers and learn from the staff how to help the pupils, while improving their understanding of the educational process and the school (Noy, 1984; Jowett and Baginsky, 1988).

In addition, involvement in their child's education may help the parents to develop their own personalities and satisfy their needs. In the school they may find an outlet for their talents and tendencies that are not used in other places. They gain satisfaction from the experience of expressing their needs and skills, from the new opportunities opened to them for self expression and realisation, and from the chance to share in the educational process and the gratitude and praise they receive for their participation and involvement (Noy, 1984; Hituv, 1989).

Teachers benefit from the parents' participation in the educational work in the school. Noy (1984) reports on four main areas in which parental involvement makes a substantial contribution: physical help, connections and contacts, the educational sphere, and creativity. Noy stresses that the great benefit that teachers draw from co-operation with parents is mainly emotional support, which helps to reduce burn-out, strengthens the teachers' professional, social and personal image, relieves the feeling of solitude that accompanies the teachers' work and increases their motivation to persevere and refresh their professional knowledge. Guidance is given on the key principles in communicating and working in partnership with parents within the revised CoP (DfES, 2001a):

- Positive attitudes to parents, user-friendly information and procedures and awareness of support needs are important.

- To make communications effective professionals should:

  - acknowledge and draw on parental knowledge and expertise

  - focus on the children's strengths as well as areas of additional need

  - recognise the personal and emotional investment of parents and be aware of their feelings

  - ensure that parents understand procedures, are aware of how to access support and are given documents to be discussed well before meetings

  - respect the validity of differing perspectives and seek constructive ways of reconciling different viewpoints

  - respect the differing needs parents themselves may have, such as a disability, or communication and linguistic barriers

  - recognise the need for flexibility in the timing and structure of meetings.

- Importantly, LEAs and schools should always seek parental permission before referring them to others for support. Where parents do not wish to have their details passed on to third parties their wishes should be respected.

Further, the statutory assessment process can be difficult and challenging for parents. Parents should be fully involved in the discussion leading up to a school's decision to require a statutory assessment.

KEY QUESTIONS

■ How does your school encourage parents to participate in the education of their child?

■ Is your school welcoming to all who visit?

■ Does your school have a home–school contract?

■ Do parents have a voice within the school community?

Section Four: Case studies

Managers and practitioners should be encouraged to extend the repertoire of their experiences beyond the classroom. The following case studies provide examples of practice that have engaged professional and parents in the common goal of preparing pupils for their role in society.

KEY QUESTIONS

■ How can schools provide resources to encourage community activities?

■ What leadership and management skills can schools provide for the broader community?

■ How can your school become an extended school (DfES, 2004a)?

■ What activities within your school could be extended to involve more members of the school community?

Case Study One: Family Connections – a programme for parents and their pre-school children

The Family Nurturing Network (FNN) is a registered charity which is part funded by social services, the pre-school teacher counselling service and an educational psychologist in a middle England city. All participants have combined their skills in order to support children and their parents.

Within the FNN, the Family Connections programme is aimed at families where the pre-school child is showing signs of developmental, emotional or behavioural disturbance of clinical severity which can undermine successful transition to school. These children are likely to have experienced some or all of the following: lack of stimulation, inconsistent and ineffective discipline, lack of good shared experience, parental hostility and rejection, violence in the home, corporal punishment, and parental absences and mental illness. They may also suffer from undetected sensory or physiological impairments. If not addressed, the child's problems and related detrimental style of parenting will continue, which are known to reduce the child's potential to benefit from education, to relate to peers and to become well-adjusted adults. For example, 50 per cent of pre-school children showing behavioural, emotional and social difficulties at home go on to present these problems in primary school. Therefore, the strategic approach to the prevention of behavioural, emotional and social difficulties in schools needs to start at the pre-school stage.

The Family Connections programme is designed to help parents of pre-school children who are showing early signs of Behavioural, Emotional and Social Difficulties (BESD) to develop more effective parenting skills, to enhance children's ability to play and communicate, and to provide baseline assessment of children coming into school. Parents learn about the principles of play and praise, how to set limits, how to deal with misbehaviour without resorting to harsh or punitive measures, and how to develop communication and problem-solving in families. These principles and skills are illustrated in a series of videos showing parents and children in everyday situations 'doing it right' and 'doing it wrong' and what effect this has on the child's behaviour and feelings. Participants watch and discuss the videos and then practise the principles in role-plays with each other during the sessions and with their children during assigned home activities between the sessions. Throughout the programme, the team emphasise that there is usually more than one way to solve a problem. Parents need to have realistic expectations of their children and be aware that each child has a unique temperament. The team also encourage parents to stop and think before responding instinctively in conflict situations, so that they develop a set of skills for use in the future and feel empowered to help their children learn and be confident.

Children are provided with a range of activities in a well-equipped nursery setting. They are encouraged to play and explore these activities with support of an adult according to individual needs. Activities are adapted to suit the children's developmental needs. When the parents join in for the last thirty minutes of each session, there is an excellent opportunity to observe, encourage, praise and give advice on play activities.

The parents' group is led by a clinical psychologist/co-ordinator of the FNN and a co-leader, often a health visitor, wishing to develop further her/his skills in assisting families. The children's group is planned, run and supervised by pre-school teacher counsellors who guide several volunteer 'key workers' specifically trained for their role with the children. An educational psychologist co-ordinates observational assessment of children and preparation of reports for parents.

The families came from very varied social and educational backgrounds; however, this was not found to be detrimental in any way to forming a very supportive group. Many parents were at the end of their tether, trying to do their best but not succeeding with their children. Often, their relationship with their children had broken down and they felt they did not have much affection left for them. They were very keen to find out first of all how to control the children, but they did readily accept that we should begin by concentrating on strengthening the attachment with the children through play. The team found that the parents often had inappropriate/unclear expectations of their children and erred by being either too harsh and punitive or too permissive instead of authoritative (not authoritarian). All participants valued the programme: parents, children and the FNN.

<table>
<tr><td colspan="1" align="center">KEY QUESTIONS</td></tr>
</table>

▪ Do family nurturing practices take place within your community, e.g. Sure Start, Family Centres, Family Nurturing Networks and Family Connections?
▪ How does your school relate to such agencies? (See also Chapter 6.)
▪ Could, or should, your school encourage parents to seek guidance and help through such agencies??

Case Study Two: Music and inclusion

Since the 1978 Warnock Report identified the needs of pupils who had restricted access to education in mainstream settings as 'special', educators have responded to the political and social drive towards inclusion. Allan and Cope (2002, p. 1) describe how this happens in practice:

> *... social inclusion has been dictated by policy imperatives which specify an increase in numbers of students present (DfEE, 1997) or reduction in the numbers of children formally assessed as having special educational needs ... as adequate measures of success.*

Pressure has been placed on researchers and practitioners to produce models of good practice which can be generalised across schools for the use of as many teachers as possible. In practice, this has led to the publication of several guides for teachers on how to respond to children with SEN. This case study examines the use of community music for inclusion. The term 'community music' refers to any collective music-making activity initiated by members of the community. The word community can signify people living within a certain locality, representing a diversity of socio-economic backgrounds; different cultures, languages and religions may also be represented within this group. In practice, most community music groups have memberships that are consistent in their shared concern and performance of music.

This case study is set in two locations, England and Portugal. In 1980, Sonia Blandford had been appointed to a large co-educational 11–18 comprehensive school located in a light industrial town in Southern England. Initial community music started with a choir for pupils and children from neighbouring schools and led to the formation of a school wind band which evolved into a Community Music Centre (CMC). Twenty years on, in Portugal, Stephanie Duarte was researching the impact of community music-making on participants. In 2001, Blandford and Duarte sought the views of past and present young musicians and their parents through a series of questionnaires and interviews over a period of six months.

The Portuguese music centre was established by Duarte and her colleagues in 1991. Located among the international community in Lisbon, the centre provides an opportunity for young people to join a musical ensemble that rehearses in languages with which participants are most familiar, i.e. English and Portuguese. The centre sympathises with the internationally mobile student and caters for students from a variety of musical backgrounds. As a community group, the International Music Centre (IMC) is unrestricted by involvement in the national music system and open to all; it caters for different levels of ability on orchestral instruments, recorder, keyboard, drum kit and guitar. To generate an income the IMC gives concerts on a regular basis in Lisbon and the Algarve.

Likewise, the CMC is open to any willing participant between 5 and 25. In its 23-year history, the CMC has sustained a membership of 150 forming three windbands and a choir. The centre provides instruments and tuition funded by grants and concerts in France, Germany and throughout the United Kingdom. Interestingly, the young musicians are taught by other members, not necessarily older, in a pattern similar to the Victorian monitor system. Members have also had the opportunity to perform with groups from America, Canada and Australia.

Inclusion through music – the benefits

It is axiomatic that the involvement of children in music-making from diverse social settings derives great benefit to all participants: performers, teachers and parents. Specifically, analysis of findings from questionnaires, group interviews and telephone and internet interviews found that community music-making was beneficial in:

1. *Development of responsibility*: the ability to talk about the music and share the experience with other students leads on to the social aspects of ensemble playing, as did the guidance given by peers.

2. *Choice of instrument*: neither cost or availability were inhibitors to participants who derived a great deal of pleasure from playing their instrument and chose to learn an instrument in anticipation of the sheer joy of performing. Many of the students opted for their instrument because of the appearance or its sound. Students gave reasons such as relaxation and concentration as to why they learnt a musical instrument.

3. *Development of ensemble skills*: both the CMC and IMC had a history of participating in music festivals mainly for fun but also to raise attainment. The participants felt that emphasis on standards regardless of individual ability was a positive reason for playing.

4. *Social inclusion*: many children from differing backgrounds have participated in the wind bands and choirs.

Table 3.1 shows how pupils reacted to the question 'Why join?' and findings were consistent for both organisations. The following comments show how young people can experience inclusion in the positive sense of the term, i.e. 'to be included'.

Table 3.1 Pupils' comments

Features	Responses
Making new friends	*'You get to know people you would otherwise not meet either because they're not at your own school or because they are not in your social circle.'* *'We've just come to this country and it's a good way to meet people and make friends.'*
Finding new friends	*'It gives me more contact with different nationalities.'* *'There is a high level of student mobility, so there are always new people to meet every year.'*
Learning about the locality	*'I don't attend this school, so the environment is new to me.'*
Adapting to a new environment	*'It has helped me to settle more quickly in this country.'* *Participating in this group helps them adapt to a new environment.*
Teamwork	*'You get to work with students from different schools.'* *'We have helped with fundraising for the centre.'* *'There is no rivalry in music.'*
Helping you to work as a team	*'There is a strong team feeling on trips and tours which is hard to experience elsewhere.'* *'I've found it especially beneficial to receive help with my parts from another member of the group.'* *'It's great to share the performing experience with others.'* *'People help each other to get over their nervousness.'*
Social interaction	*'It's interesting to meet people from different cultures and ages.'* *'It's great for holidays and trips!'*

With the CMC, there are several examples illustrating the inclusion of children with SEN of which the following are just two:

■ When the CMC first met Lynette, she was five years old, legs in callipers and hands clasped close to her body; she had been mentally and physically disabled since birth. Abandoned by her family she had been institutionalised in the North of England and eventually moved to Wiltshire. The CMC met Lynette at a Christmas concert to her 'family' in the 'home'. After three such visits, it became apparent that she had a particular interest in music and soon afterwards she was invited to join the CMC. Several weeks later Lynette joined the percussion section. During the following twelve years, she participated in concerts at home and abroad. Her hands and legs developed so that, by the age of 18, she had shed the callipers and developed social skills to enable her to find employment in a local store. Sadly, at the age of 20, Lynette was relocated and could no longer participate; but in the twelve-year period of her association with the CMC all manner of children engaged with her musically and socially, without any inappropriate or negative comments.

Chris was born with a severe hearing impairment. Through attending his brother's music lessons, he was provided with the opportunity to pick up a euphonium. Within weeks he was able to play a tune and months later joined the beginner's wind band. His lack of hearing was not a problem, he could follow the beat and would be guided by his neighbour as to what piece and which section he should be playing during rehearsal. In 1997 Chris joined the Trinity College of Music as a Junior Exhibitionist.

What conclusions?

Blandford and Duarte (2002) found that the social benefits motivated and sustained memberships of their centres. Social skills are enhanced by participation in a musical community through the development of friendships, improved self-confidence and in many cases, facilitated transition into a new environment.

In terms of learning, participants developed transferable skills associated with behaviour to learn and responsibility. Through teaching and guiding younger members the participants were able to gain understanding of their own needs particularly in the areas of intonation, aural perception, notation and ensemble proficiency. The experience of inclusion moves beyond notions of class, ability, race or creed and has been demonstrated by research, practice and music-making. In terms of inclusion, it would appear that by moving out of school and into the community the codes that limit our understanding of community are broken.

Participation in a musical community is fully inclusive. Children with learning and physical disabilities are supported and stimulated by the group. Students from different nationalities, cultural backgrounds, abilities and a wide age range are able to combine their efforts to the common good of the community. All players reported how much they had enjoyed the experience of participating in a musical community. As reflected in the words of the music educator Isaac Stern (Guaspari, 1999; p. 149), the aim of music-making is:

> ... *not to make 'musicians' out of everyday performers, but more important, to make them educated, alert, caring inquiring young people, who by playing music feel a part of the connective tissue between what the mind of man has been able to devise and the creativity of music ... in other words, become literate, and part of the culture of the whole world.*

Having read the case studies, what can you do to improve your school and relationships with members of the school and local community?

TO DO	ACTION

Executive summary

■ To be inclusive, every school has to become a community within a community.

■ All members of the school should be encouraged to have a shared commitment to the creation of the school community.

■ Within the context of community, it is necessary to consider how education contributes to the life-long experience of its members.

■ Community can be defined in terms of location, structure and process:

  – where it is, the influence of the environment and systems of control

  – the administrative elements and guidance that determine equality of provision

  – the management of people and development of a shared understanding of beliefs and values.

■ An understanding of the culture of schools is required before considering the management of SEN. The culture of each school is determined by individual and collective beliefs and values.

■ The interpersonal relationships create the ethos, the shared beliefs and values. The whole-school feeling exists to such an extent that it drives the school as a community towards achieving goals.

■ There is a distinctive link between the atmosphere created in schools and their environment.

■ According to Durkheim, the purpose of education is to create the social entity, i.e. socialisation of the individual from the moment of birth.

■ Parents and schools need to do everything they can to help their children relate co-operatively to adults and other children.

■ Community activities should be encouraged within the extended school community.

Further reading

Dewey, J. (1960), *Democracy and Education – Introduction to the Philosophy of Education. Classics in World Literature*, Jerusalem, Hebrew University of Jerusalem and Bialik Institute. (Hebrew translation)
Durkheim, E. (1967), *Education and Sociology*, New York: The Free Press
Poster, C. (1982), *Community Education*, London: Heinemann

From the Community to the Classroom

CHAPTER 4: KEY QUESTIONS TO BE CONSIDERED
■ How can teachers be inclusive practitioners?
■ What skills are involved?
■ When and where do practitioners develop these skills?
■ Where and from whom can practitioners seek support?
■ How can the Acknowledge Understand Provide for model underpin practice in schools?

Introduction

This chapter will provide practical suggestions and a guide to enable the practitioner to implement the theory of inclusion in the classroom. This focuses on **Acknowledging** SEN or disability, while **Understanding** the individual nature of subsequent learning needs and on the basis of professional knowledge, CPD and school support mechanisms, implementing practical strategies which **Provide for** the learner (**AUP**). The AUP model recognises the importance of education for all, as Stainback et al. (1994, p. 489) state:

> *... the goal of inclusion is not to erase differences but to enable all students to belong within an educational community that validates and values their individuality.*

This chapter provides an insight into the practical applications of inclusion in the mainstream classroom setting. Chapter 4 is presented in three sections:

- ■ Section One: A new approach to learning and teaching
- ■ Section Two: The Special Educational Needs Co-ordinator (SENCO) and SEN team
- ■ Section Three: The AUP practitioner.

Section One: A new approach to learning and teaching

Since the 1960s, classroom practice has been influenced by the child-centred theories of Piaget, Montessori and Froebel. This emphasises a need for teachers to reflect on classroom organisation and approaches to learning and teaching. Solity (1992, p. 9) provides a useful summary:

> *The classroom is then geared to stimulate children, to encourage interest and of their learning to be based on their experiences. The teacher is a facilitator, promoting learning and acting as the child's guide in the learning process.*

However, an emphasis on child-centred education might lead to a deficit model of special education. This happens if the teacher assesses the child's learning in a negative fashion. Within the orthodox model of child-centred education, there is a need for the teacher to provide a remedy to poor cognitive and social abilities, as determined by comparing pupils with SEN to peer group average levels. Solity (1992, p. 9) comments:

> *A failure to learn was closely associated with faulty intellectual development. … Some of the limitations of child-centred education could be seen as:*
> - *the implications when children fail*
> - *the difficulties of successfully implementing the philosophy in the classroom*
> - *the problems of letting children develop at their own rate.*

This chapter focuses on an approach to learning which recognises the learner's needs within the context of an outcome-driven curriculum. As stated, the approach for practitioners is Acknowledge Understand and Provide for (AUP).

Acknowledge SEN or disability
Understand Individual learning needs
Provide Support for learning and teaching

The initial question is how to make education more responsive to an individual child or how to deliver personalised learning. This means:

- having high expectations of all children

- building on the knowledge, interests and aptitudes of every child

- involving children in their own learning through shared objectives and feedback

- helping children to become confident learners

- enabling children to develop the skills they will need beyond school.

Personalised learning embraces every aspect of school life including teaching and learning strategies, Information Communication Technology (ICT), curriculum choice, organisation and timetabling, assessment arrangements and relationships with the local community. Effective teaching for children deemed as having SEN shares most of the characteristics of effective teaching for all children. As schools become more inclusive, teachers must be able to respond to a wider range of needs in the classroom. To support them in this task, there is a need to sharpen the focus on children with SEN within the National Strategies and through action to improve Initial Teacher Education, induction and professional development opportunities.

Social context and relationship management in the classroom

Developing good learning relationships is fundamental to effective teaching. Moreover, learning behaviours are integrated components of the classroom rather than fragmented attributes of the child (Cornwall and Tod, 1998). The social context of the classroom has long been researched and the importance of wider influences on learners' behaviour should not be ignored. Case study research suggests that the quality of the relationship between teacher and learner is very significant (Cline, 1992). Further research (Serow and Solomon, 1979; Prawat and Nickerson, 1985) suggests that children are more likely to develop positive attitudes and behaviours when they experience positive relationships with their teachers. Teachers' self-perception of their skills and confidence is an important consideration for relationships management in the classroom. A consequence of lack of confidence could result in less skilled teaching and increased disaffection and challenging behaviour in the classroom.

Active learning of the kind that is to be encouraged, if learners are to be motivated and take responsibility for their own achievements, asks learners to be self-motivated and collaborate with others to construct their knowledge. Moll and Whitmore (1998) describe the teacher's roles as guide and supporter, active participant in learning, evaluator and facilitator.

All of these activities are part of the relationship between teacher and learner, but there are many less definable or measurable facets to the relationship, such as the ability to encourage the learner or providing responsive instruction. Castelijns (1996) states that responsive instruction is typified by teachers showing that they:

- are available for support and instruction

- are willing to take the learner's perspective on work problems

- are willing to support the learner's competencies

- will challenge the student to be active and responsible in choosing, planning, executing and evaluating the activity and its outcomes.

Involving learners in the planning of their study or learning objectives is not a new strategy and was reaffirmed in the revised CoP (DfES, 2001a). The benefits to learners range from ownership of targets to more accurate judgements, and hence assessment, of their own performance (Munby, 1994). To achieve this kind of learner involvement pre-supposes an encouraging relationship between teacher and learner.

Relationships with peers are also considered to be important factors in school learning. In recent years an emphasis on inclusive environments has resulted in increased mixed ability classrooms and schools. Research indicates that traditional whole-class instruction, which is teacher-directed to all class members with uniform academic tasks and ways of performing, is inappropriate as a primary mode of instruction in heterogeneous classes since it fails to cope with the differences between pupils in terms of needs and abilities (Ben-Ari and Shafir, 1988). Vygotsky (1962) emphasised the pivotal contribution of social interaction to cognitive development and the view that cognitive development is a process of continuous interplay between the individual and the environment. It follows that classroom groupings for teaching and peer relationships could have a significant impact on learning. It is important for teachers to recognise and foster the possible mechanisms for improved learning behaviour (Hertz-Lazarowitz and Miller, 1992). The lack of appropriate social and interpersonal skills and competencies can result from any home background so it is necessary to enhance positive learning behaviours by encouraging:

- high feelings of self-worth

- a robust sense of self

- self-reliance

- autonomy

- a positive view of the world

- a sense of personal power.

Much has been written about classroom practice. The following text is taken from *Key Stage 3 Strategy* (DfES, 2003b) and provides succinct guidance to managers and practitioners in mainstream settings.

> *Classroom Organisation concerns substantially more than furniture arrangement, displays of pupils' work and the use and choice of equipment. It includes consideration of pupil groupings and the use of other adults, whether teachers, teaching assistants or other helpers. Decisions about classroom organisations need to support interactivity; and teachers need to be conscious of the impact of different social settings on effective learning. Over the next year, the Strategy will provide further advice on these aspects of classroom organisation.*
>
> *A process of lesson design ... illustrates how the design sequence incorporates the features already considered. It also emphasises the advice that successful lesson design should be viewed as a series of planned learning episodes.*

Locate the lesson or sequence of lessons in the context of:

- *the scheme of work;*
- *pupils' prior knowledge;*
- *pupils' preferred learning styles.*

Identify clearly the essential objective(s) for pupils in terms of:

- *their knowledge, understanding and skills;*
- *their attitudes and personal development.*

Structure the lesson as a series of episodes by:

- *separating the learning into distinct stages or steps.*

Decide how to teach each episode, then choose:

- *the best pedagogic approach;*
- *the most appropriate teaching and learning strategies;*
- *the most effective organisation for each episode.*

Ensure coherence by providing:

- *a stimulating start to the lesson;*
- *transition between episodes which recapitulate and launch new episodes;*
- *a final plenary that reviews learning.*

Detailed lesson planning is of vital importance but it should not be seen as a straitjacket. Successful teachers are alert to the responses of their pupils and make modifications and adjustments to meet the evolving dynamics of each lesson.

Creating inclusive classrooms

The following practical suggestions are taken from Cheminais (2004). They provide a good framework for inclusive teaching and learning:

1. *A welcoming, friendly, supportive and emotionally literate classroom climate is of prime importance; where pupils and staff feel secure, are able to share feelings and ask questions; where misunderstandings are dealt with sensitively, and used as positive teaching points; where put-downs are not permitted, and where SEN pupils' strengths and talents are valued, celebrated and incorporated within lessons.*

2.   *Teachers and teaching assistants who have high expectations, making these clear to pupils, and incorporating the learning cycle structure in all lessons. This entails establishing a positive mind-set and readiness for learning; connecting pupils' previous learning to new learning; giving pupils the big picture, sharing the lesson objectives and expected outcomes with pupils; breaking learning down into achievable steps, as well as providing extension activities, utilising multi-sensory teaching and learning approaches; ensuring pupils are active participants throughout the lesson; providing opportunities for pupils to demonstrate their knowledge and understanding, and to review and reflect upon their learning at the end of the lesson, in order to ensure new knowledge is not lost.*

3.   *The teacher and teaching assistant modelling effective learning strategies and expected outcomes. This would also entail pupils being provided with a range of learning and curriculum access resources that would enable them to extend their research and study skills, and to produce learning outcomes in a variety of alternative formats, in ICT, digital technology, multimedia, as a regular feature of lessons.*

4.   *Providing opportunities for pupils to talk about their learning, e.g. describing the different ways they talked through a problem; asking open questions to prompt alternative solutions and approaches; and ensuring that pupils work in a variety of ways, in pairs and small groups, as a whole class or independently, during the lesson.*

5.   *Encouraging pupils to assess their own learning and that of their peers sensitively and constructively; teachers commenting on pupils' work, indicating clearly what each pupil needs to do in order to improve, or make their next piece of work of 'premier league' quality.*

6.   *Teaching assistants being empowered to utilise their strengths; being clear about their role in relation to the effectiveness of their VAK (Visual, Auditory, Kinaesthetic) support strategies, in consolidating and extending pupils' learning. Teaching assistants who can differentiate 'on the spot' using both hi-tech and lo-tech aids, are a powerful learning resource.*

KEY QUESTIONS

In assisting with this process, practitioners might consider the following questions:

■   What do you understand by the term 'inclusive teaching and learning'?

■   Are you already experienced in working with pupils who have disability/SEN?

■   Do you feel comfortable with the type of reflective practice required to support all pupils?

■   What skills do you already have? What skills do you feel lacking in? Further guidance on professional development can be found in Chapter 8.

Section Two: The Special Educational Needs Co-ordinator and SEN team

Much of the responsibility for pupils with SEN resides with the SENCO and the SEN team. As stated in Chapter 2 with the initial Code of Practice (DfE, 1994a), the SENCO emerged as a statutory role in mainstream and special schools. The CoP was the response by government to provide schools with guidance on how to manage the learning needs of all pupils in a way that promoted inclusion. The role of SENCO involves a range of responsibilities including that of INSET provider and supporting the CPD of classroom teachers so they felt willing and able to work in an inclusive classroom.

For all primary or secondary classroom teachers, it is important to grasp the significance and individual nature of their school's SEN provision. Provision for pupils with SEN transcends all aspects of the school's pastoral and academic life; however, to expect one person (SENCO) to carry such a mammoth task is often impracticable. There is the potential for a concentrated workload to lead to stress that could stagnate the development of inclusive communities (Gibson, 2001a; Thomas and Loxley, 2001).

In the revised CoP (DfES, 2001a), guidance is provided on how the SEN team can support colleagues who are finding inclusion problematic. In particular the CoP promotes the social model of disability in suggesting that practitioners do not react to a perceived deficit in a pupil's ability to learn more, but take a broader look at the social factors impacting on the pupil's ability to learn. Furthermore they are encouraged to draw support from colleagues within a SEN team designated to deal with issues throughout the school. As Rose (2001, p. 148) explains:

> *... an obstacle for inclusion is the emphasis which the current education system places upon the difficulties presented by the child with SEN rather than on the development of strategies and classroom practices which would enable inclusion to be achieved.*

Critical thinking and professional reflection are essential to an effective practitioner. In supporting the development of such skills, teachers need access to CPD or INSET. It is the role of the SENCO and/or the SEN team to ensure this provision is available. The SEN team as outlined in Chapter 2 will include SENCO and where established deputy SENCO, representatives from senior and middle management, a sample of scool teachers (faculty based or key stage based depending on primary or secondary setting), Teaching Assistants, the governing body and when possible parents and pupils.

Teaching Assistants

The Teaching Assistant (TA) has become a valuable resource in primary and secondary education, providing support for pupils, teachers, curriculum and school (Blanning, 2004). The role of the TA has expanded dramatically over the past decade so that they are no longer regarded as the helper but someone who is actively involved with the teaching and learning of young people. One of their qualities is that most are experienced parents who recognise and are aware of the complex and diverse needs of young people. They are able to communicate with pupils effectively on an academic or personal level. However, there is controversy in the way that TAs are perceived. They do not claim to be the teacher and follow the structure of the lesson as set by the teacher, but they are able with collaboration to differentiate work for students to suit their educational needs and learning. TAs require training to meet the needs of the pupils in their care; practitioners also require training in the management of support staff. The following extract is taken from *Barriers to Inclusion* (DfES, 2004a, p. 60) and relates to the role of TAs who work with pupils with SEN:

- *Teaching assistants play a valuable role, providing one-to-one support to children with SEN as well as wider support in the classroom.*

- *Individual support from a TA can in some cases lead to less involvement by the teacher, leaving the TA to deliver most of the curriculum.*

- *It is important that teachers and TAs play complementary roles so children do not rely excessively on the TA or solely on one-to-one help.*

- *If they are supported to learn within peer groups, they will be better able to develop social and collaborative skills enabling them to move towards increasingly independent learning.*

ACTIVITY 4.1: EFFECTIVE USE OF TEACHING ASSISTANTS

Practitioners should consider the following questions in relation to their school's use of Teaching Assistants:

- How can teachers and TAs collaborate in the classroom?

- How is full and active participation by pupils encouraged?

- How can TAs be used in a way that utilises their skills, supports the teacher and the pupils?

- Is it both appropriate and possible for TAs to be affiliated to subject teams/faculties/key stage groups?

- How can teachers and TAs work in planning lessons together?

- How are lessons planned with regard to differentiation?

- What support services are available to all pupils?

Section Three: The AUP practitioner

It is axiomatic that the practitioner in mainstream classrooms works in a radically different environment compared to the early 1990s. Table 4.1 indicates there is no such thing as a definitive guide to managing and teaching pupils with SEN. Such an endeavour needs to stem from teachers with reflective thinking in collaboration with the pupil, TA, SENCO and SEN team and in all cases parents or guardians.

Tables 4.2 to 4.13 provide guidance on how to manage disabilities in the inclusive classroom. Each should provide practitioners with a range of guidance on development as an AUP practitioner. Each table addresses a specific disability or SEN, providing information on the symptoms as well as suggestions on classroom and curriculum organisation. Finally the tables detail how to work with support staff and other relevant organisations as well as web-sites for further research and information. The following list of SEN and disabilities is taken from OfSTED documentation but is not exhaustive; there are other types of disability and SEN which practitioners may come into contact with as an AUP practitioner.

- Asperger's Syndrome (Table 4.2)

- Autistic Spectrum Disorders (Table 4.3)

- Behavioural, Emotional and Social Difficulties (Table 4.4)

- Cerebral Palsy (Table 4.5)

- Cystic Fibrosis (Table 4.6)

- Down's Syndrome (Table 4.7)

- Dyslexia (Table 4.8)

- English as an Additional Language (Table 4.9)

- Hearing Impairment (Table 4.10)

- Multiple Sclerosis (Table 4.11)

- Speech, Language and Communication Difficulties (Table 4.12)

- Visual Impairment (Table 4.13).

Table 4.1 Theories of inclusive education practice

Lawson (2002, p. 18)	*In March 2001, QCA [Qualification and Curriculum Authority] published a set of booklets/non-statutory guidelines for* Planning, teaching and assessing the curriculum for pupils with learning difficulties ... *This framework formed a researched basis for the development of the performance descriptors (P Levels) which chart progress up to Level 1 through eight steps.*
Sebba and Sachdev (1997, p. 75)	*The factor that has the greatest impact upon a school's ability to become inclusive are the expectations of staff, parents and the pupils themselves.*
Rouse and Agbenu (1998, p. 81)	*Analysing the learning environment as an approach to the assessment of special needs does not prescribe particular forms of assessment, but does recognise the importance of the involvement of teachers in the assessment process and values the information teachers have about their students ... Proponents of this view stress the need for students to play an active role in their own assessments.*
Rouse and Agbenu (1998, p. 86)	*Specific feedback is more effective than giving pupils a grade or position relative to others.*
Rose, (2001, p. 155)	*Teachers should have a good opportunity both to debate the issues and to be provided with examples of good practice that demonstrate how schools have addressed their concerns.*
OfSTED (2004a, p. 6)	*Target setting has the greatest impact when it focuses on precise curriculum objectives for individuals and when it forms part of a whole school improvement process.*

Table 4.2 AUP for Asperger's Syndrome in the primary and secondary classroom

General symptoms	▨ Choose to work and be alone. ▨ Need routine and to know exactly what is expected from them. ▨ Communication difficulties with a tendency to interpret meaning literally. ▨ Inability to understand subtlety or irony. ▨ A tendency towards Obsessive Compulsive Behaviour. ▨ Limited organisational abilities.
Suggestions for inclusive and effective classroom management	▨ Structure tasks well and ensure instructions are made available orally, visually and in writing. ▨ Ensure you have the pupil's attention throughout and that they fully understand what is expected of them. Make use of TA to assist. ▨ Liaise regularly with SENCO and TA in planning lessons and ensuring provision is made to manage behaviour. ▨ If needed, obtain input and support from an educational psychologist accessed via SENCO.
Organisations and web-sites to access further information	Asperger's Syndrome: A Developmental Puzzle www.practicalparent.org.uk/asper.htm Asperger's Syndrome www.paains.org.uk/related/aspergers.htm Asperger's Syndrome Information Sources www.btinternet.com/~black.ice/addnet/aspergers.html Planning, teaching and assessing the curriculum for pupils with learning difficulties http://www.nc.uk.net/ld/index.html

Table 4.3 AUP for Autistic Spectrum Disorders in the primary and secondary classroom

General symptoms	Triad of impairments: ■ **Social interaction**: difficulty with social relationships, appearing remote to others. ■ **Social communication**: difficulty with verbal and non-verbal communication. Inability to detect and/or understand irony, sarcasm, wit. A tendency to take meaning literally. ■ **Imagination**: difficulty in playing with others and using imagination and or creativity.
Suggestions for inclusive and effective classroom management	■ Structure tasks well and ensure instructions are made available orally, visually and in writing. ■ Ensure you have the pupil's attention throughout and make use of TA to assist. ■ Liaise regularly with SENCO and TA in planning lessons and ensuring provision is made to manage behaviour. ■ If needed, obtain input and support from an educational psychologist accessed via SENCO.
Organisations and web-sites to access further information	Autism Independent UK www.autismuk.com Autism fact sheets hcd2.bupa.co.uk/fact_sheets/html/autism.html Autism Connect www.autismconnect.org The National Autistic Society www.nas.org.uk Planning, teaching and assessing the curriculum for pupils with learning difficulties http://www.nc.uk.net/ld/index.html

Table 4.4 AUP for Behavioural, Emotional and Social Difficulties in the primary and secondary classroom

General symptoms	■ Difficulty concentrating ■ Distracting peers ■ Inattentiveness ■ Disregard for teacher and peer group ■ Regular swearing ■ Being subjected to and/or instigating bullying ■ Fighting ■ Lack of self-esteem ■ Poor appreciation of their work and others' ■ Possible vandalism of school property ■ Anxiety and/or depression.
Suggestions for inclusive and effective classroom management	■ Assign a mentor – either peer or adult. ■ Set achievable tasks to raise self-esteem. ■ Liaise with SENCO and if required parents to understand pupils' needs. ■ With TA support, devise a weekly diary to co-ordinate their tasks, progress, goals and misdemeanours. ■ Hold regular and collaborative meetings to discuss lesson planning with SENCO and ideally TA.
Organisations and web-sites to access further information	DfES www.dfes.gov.uk/sen AWCEBD www.awcebd.co.uk Education By Design www.edbydesign.org/help/help.html Advice and Assessment www.educational-psychologist.co.uk/behaviour.htm Disruptive and Disaffected pupils in Mainstream Schools www.users.globalnet.co.uk/~ebdstudy/index.htm The Learning Assistance Programme www.lap.asn.au

Table 4.5 AUP for Cerebral Palsy (CP) in the primary and secondary classroom

General symptoms	Caused by damage to and/or lack of 'normal' development in part of the brain affecting movement. Three types of CP, although some cases may exhibit symptoms from the range: <ul><li>**Spasticity**: affecting movement, muscle control and development.</li><li>**Athetosis**: causing muscle spasms and involuntary movements of the muscles.</li><li>**Ataxia**: causing much imbalance and difficulties walking.</li></ul>
Suggestions for inclusive and effective classroom management	Depending on nature and severity of pupil's CP, the following are basic guidelines. Always seek professional guidance from pupil's occupational therapist via SENCO: <ul><li>If pupil is a wheelchair user, ensure that adequate space and seating positioning is considered and provided.</li><li>If pupil has poor fine motor skills, use of a computer and assistance of a TA is recommended.</li><li>Pupils with CP can tire easily, so plan lessons accordingly, taking into consideration time of day.</li><li>Liaise regularly with SENCO and TA in planning lessons.</li></ul>
Organisations and web-sites to access further information	Cerebral Palsy Facts www.cerebralpalsyfacts.com SCOPE www.scope.org.uk Disability World www.disabilityworld.com

Table 4.6 AUP for Cystic Fibrosis (CF) in the primary and secondary classroom

General symptoms	A genetic disease affecting the lungs and pancreas. ■ Causes the build up of mucus in the lungs and digestive system. ■ Narrowing of airways causing difficulties in breathing. ■ Pancreas prevented from secreting necessary digestive enzymes due to thickened mucus in the digestive system. ■ Persistent coughing. ■ Regular colds and/or chest infections. ■ Anxiety and/or depression.
Suggestions for inclusive and effective classroom management	Depending on severity of pupil's CF, the following are basic guidelines. Always seek professional guidance from pupil's physiotherapist via your SENCO: ■ Pupils with CF need regular physiotherapy through the day to assist in clearing the lungs. Ensure you plan lessons with this in mind. ■ Ensure you know where your pupil's nebuliser is located if needed during the day. ■ Pupils with CF tire easily, so plan lessons accordingly, taking into consideration time of day. ■ Liaise regularly with SENCO and TA in planning lessons.
Organisations and web-sites to access further information	Cystic Fibrosis www.goodgulf.com/cystic.html Cystic Fibrosis www.cysticfibrosis.com

63

Table 4.7 AUP for Down's Syndrome in the primary and secondary classroom

General symptoms	<ul><li>Short stature</li><li>Slanting eyes</li><li>Poor muscle tone</li><li>Short-term memory problems</li><li>Hearing loss</li><li>Heart defects</li><li>Visual difficulties</li><li>Gastro-intestinal conditions.</li></ul>
Suggestions for inclusive and effective classroom management	<ul><li>Careful and regular assessment with SENCO, external agencies and parents.</li><li>Simplify instructions and tasks.</li><li>Information provided in smaller components.</li><li>Regular and collaborative meetings re. lesson planning with SENCO and ideally TA.</li><li>Ensure pupil has full visual access to board and teacher.</li></ul>
Organisations and web-sites to access further information	Teaching Strategies and Techniques www.ldonline.org/ld_indepth/teaching_techniques/strategies.html Mail-base for SEN Teachers and SENCOs www.mailbase.ac.uk/category/X6.html UK Resources for Down's Syndrome www.43green.freeserve.co.uk/uk_downs_syndrome/ukdsinfo.html The Down's Syndrome Association www.downs-syndrome.org.uk Planning, teaching and assessing the curriculum for pupils with learning difficulties http://www.nc.uk.net/ld/index.html

Table 4.8 AUP for Dyslexia in the primary and secondary classroom

General symptoms	■ Difficulty with speech development with tendency to jumble phrases ■ Poor concentration ■ Reverses words and letters ■ Difficulty writing, spelling and reading ■ Short-term memory difficulties ■ Right/Left confusion ■ May have poor fine and/or gross motor skills ■ Trouble organising thoughts and sequencing ideas on paper ■ Poor general organisational skills.
Suggestions for inclusive and effective classroom management	■ Provide alternative means of recording information. ■ Use Information Technology (IT), e.g. voice recognition software. ■ Provide extra time for completing written tasks both in classroom and homework. ■ Give one instruction at a time. ■ Allow sufficient time for processing verbal instruction. ■ Use visual and kinaesthetic teaching. ■ Hold regular and collaborative meetings to determine lesson planning with SENCO and Ideally TA.
Organisations and web-sites to access further information	DfES www.dfes.gov.uk/sen The British Dyslexia Association www.bda-dyslexia.org.uk Dyslexia Teacher www.dyslexia-teacher.com The Dyslexia Institute www.dyslexia-inst.org.uk

Table 4.9 AUP for English as an Additional Language (EAL) in the primary and secondary classroom

General symptoms	Children from families that do not speak English at home and need assistance in accessing services and support. The following characteristics are basic indictors of pupils with EAL: ■ Not speaking English after exposure to it for six months or more ■ Difficulty staying on task ■ Isolation from peer group ■ Difficulties in most curriculum subjects ■ Anxiety and/or depression ■ Subjected to and/or instigator of bullying ■ Behavioural, Emotional and Social Difficulties.
Suggestions for inclusive and effective classroom management	If pupil has 'asylum seeker' or 'refugee' status, your headteacher and/or SENCO will have made contact with the Ethnic Minority Achievement Service and located the pupil's named support worker: ■ Use multi-sensory teaching approaches (e.g. signs and symbols, visual materials, audio and ICT) to support pupil's understanding and subsequent communication with teacher and peer group. ■ Praise efforts and successes of the pupil. ■ Be gentle in any necessary disapproval. ■ Build upon pupil's previous knowledge and interests. ■ Keep a log with TA of pupil's language and communication development. ■ Liaise regularly with SENCO and TA in planning lessons.
Organisations and web-sites to access further information	The Education of Asylum Seeker Pupils www.ofsted.gov.uk DfES www.dfes.gov.uk/sen The assessment of pupils with EAL www.standards.dfee.gov.uk/midbins/keystage3/EAL_09.PDF National Association for Language Development in the Curriculum www.naldic.org.uk BECTA ICT advice www.ictadvice.org.uk/index.php?section=tl&rid=1801&catcode=as_inc_sup_03

Table 4.10 AUP for Hearing Impairment (HI) in the primary and secondary classroom

General symptoms	Varies depending on type: **conductive** (relating to outer ear, e.g. Glue ear), **sensori-neural** (relating to inner ear, referred to as nerve deafness), or **mixed conductive/sensori-neural**.
	▪ Appearing not to understand what is being said and/or what is required
	▪ Poor speech and sentence construction
	▪ Inability to stay on task
	▪ Appearing tense or stressed
	▪ Tendency to daydream.
Suggestions for inclusive and effective classroom management	Depending on nature and severity of pupil's HI, the following are basic guidelines. Always seek professional guidance from your SENCO:
	▪ Plan lessons with pupil's aural needs in mind.
	▪ Speak clearly and slowly, ensuring you are holding pupil's attention.
	▪ Use sign language communication aids such as British Sign Language, Makaton, Picture Exchange Communication System and Electronic aids.
	▪ Ensure pupil has full vision; do not speak when turned towards board/computer.
	▪ Use your hands for appropriate gestures thus reiterating your point via another method.
	▪ Structure tasks well and ensure instructions are made available orally, visually and in writing.
	▪ Liaise regularly with SENCO and TA in planning lessons.
Organisations and web-sites to access further information	Ability www.ability.org.uk/Deaf.html Hearing Impairment www.careline.org.uk/Categories.asp?WSCAT=PhysDis%2BHearImp Deaf Club www.deafclub.co.uk

Table 4.11 AUP for Multiple Sclerosis (MS)in the primary and secondary classroom

General symptoms	Varies depending on type: **Benign**, **Secondary/ Progressive and Primary/Progressive**. ■ Tingling and or numbness of the skin and muscles ■ Difficulties with balance ■ Slurring of speech ■ Blurred and/or double vision ■ Difficulties in walking ■ Muscle weakness and/or pain ■ Muscle spasms ■ Extreme fatigue ■ Anxiety and/or depression.
Suggestions for inclusive and effective classroom management	Depending on nature and severity of pupil's MS, the following are basic guidelines. Always seek professional guidance from pupil's neurologist/physiotherapist/ occupational therapist via your SENCO: ■ If your pupil is a wheelchair user, ensure that adequate space and seating positioning is considered and provided. ■ If pupil is having difficulties with writing and/or reading, ensure computer is provided and ideally this resource accessed via assistance of a TA. ■ Pupils with MS tire easily, so plan lessons accordingly, taking into consideration time of day. ■ Liaise regularly with SENCO and TA in planning lessons.
Organisations and web-sites to access further information	Multiple Sclerosis Symptoms www.spotlighthealth.com/multiple_sclerosis/ms _overview/mssymptoms.html Educational Psychologist www.educational-psychologist.co.uk/links.htm Disability World www.disabilityworld.com

Table 4.12 AUP for Speech, Language and Communication Difficulties in the primary and secondary classroom

General symptoms	<ul><li>Difficulty with word and sentence formation, oral and written</li><li>Comprehension difficulties</li><li>Problems with expressing thoughts</li><li>Difficulty concentrating, understanding and staying on task</li><li>Reading difficulties</li><li>Right/Left confusion</li><li>Easily distracted</li><li>Impaired spatial awareness</li><li>Low self-esteem.</li></ul>
Suggestions for inclusive and effective classroom management	<ul><li>Simplify tasks and ensure that instructions are made available orally, visually and in writing.</li><li>Use sign language communication aids such as British Sign Language, Makaton, Picture Exchange Communication System and Electronic aids.</li><li>If needed, obtain input and support from a speech and language therapist accessed via SENCO.</li><li>Hold regular and collaborative meetings to determine lesson planning with SENCO and ideally TA.</li></ul>
Organisations and web-sites to access further information	ACE Centre Advisory Trust www.ace-centre.org.uk TeacherNet www.teachernet.gov.uk/wholeschool/sen Helping Children to communicate www.ican.org.uk/index.asp

Table 4.13 AUP for Visual Impairment (VI) in the primary and secondary classroom

General symptoms	Varies depending on type of VI: **Focus**: Problems with short-sightedness or long-sightedness in the main remedied with glasses or contact lenses. **Field**: This includes peripheral problems and/or within the field of vision. ■ Clumsiness ■ Rubbing of eyes ■ Complaining of dizziness and/or headaches ■ Difficulties taking information from the board/computer ■ Poor hand–eye co-ordination.
Suggestions for inclusive and effective classroom management	Depending on nature and severity of pupil's VI, the following are basic guidelines. Always seek professional guidance from your SENCO: ■ Plan lessons with pupil's visual needs in mind. ■ If appropriate provide pupil with Braille version of board work and/or use large print in handouts/books. ■ Depending on nature of VI, coloured paper (generally buff) with Arial font 12 should be used on any handouts/reading material given to the pupil. ■ Structure tasks well and ensure instructions are made available orally, visually and in writing. ■ Liaise regularly with SENCO and TA in planning lessons.
Organisations and web-sites to access further information	Ability www.ability.org.uk/blind.html Royal National Institute of the Blind (RNIB) www.rnib.org.uk/xpedio/groups/public/documents/code/InternetHome.hcsp

ACTIVITY 4.2: MEETING THE NEEDS OF ALL LEARNERS

This activity will help as practitioners review their current thinking with regards to meeting the needs of all learners in their primary and/or secondary classroom.

▪ What do you understand your role as 'teacher' to be?

▪ Are you of the view that pupils with SEN are best catered for in separate environments and if so why?

▪ Do you see mainstream education for all pupils as a positive development in light of current global moves towards social justice and equal opportunity?

▪ Are you aware of who your SENCO is and are you in any way involved in assisting with this role?

▪ Can you think of ways in which to make better use of TA support?

▪ How do you differentiate assessment of pupils below Level 1 on National Curriculum attainment levels?

▪ What if any experience do you have of using 'P-levels' and could this be shared with colleagues?

▪ Do you see yourself as an AUP practitioner or a 'Not in my Subject Area' (NIMSA) (Garner, 2000a) practitioner?

▪ With regards to including your pupils, what are your current CPD needs and have you talked to your SENCO or SEN team about these and ways in which they could be met?

This page can be photocopied. © *Managing Special Educational Needs*, Gibson and Blandford, 2005

Executive summary

▪ SEN and barriers to pupil progress exist due to a complex interplay of factors: attitudes, values, experiences and practices existing at the pupil's social, biological and educational level.

▪ In order to effectively understand and meet the needs of some learners, teachers need to adopt an interactionist approach to assessing and understanding the pupil's leaning needs, i.e. SENs need to be understood in the context in which they occur.

▪ In order to combat work-related stress for NQT, established teacher and SENCO, it is advised that a SEN team is established, chaired by the school SENCO, to manage SEN policy and CPD needs of staff.

▪ Teachers acknowledge their own learning needs and develop reflective skills as they work towards becoming an effective AUP practitioner.

■ Although there are certain recommendations for accommodating the social, environmental and learning needs of pupils with specific disabilities, it is understood that there is no such thing as a panacea in teaching pupils with SEN. Each case is as individual as is each teacher and school community and needs to be assessed, understood and provided for in context.

■ It is recommended that the pupils' and parents' or guardians' voice be listened to and their suggestions taken on board as fully as possible.

■ An understanding of SEN and disabilities will inform practice within the classroom.

Further reading

Cheminais, R. (2000), *Special Educational Needs for Newly Qualified Teachers*, London: David Fulton Publishers

Gibson, S. (2001c), *Special Educational Needs Teacher's Guide to the Internet*, Bristol: Classroom Resources

Lewis, A. and Norwich, B. (2004), *Special Teaching for Special Children*, Buckingham: Open University Press

Nind, M., Rix, J., Sheehy, K. and Simmons, K. (eds) (2003), *Inclusive Education: Diverse Perspectives*, London: David Fulton Publishers

Office for Standards in Education (OfSTED) (2004b), *Special Educational Needs and Disability, HMI 2276*, London: OfSTED Publications

Leadership and Management

5

CHAPTER 5: KEY QUESTIONS TO BE CONSIDERED
■ What is leadership within an inclusive school?
■ How do leaders manage an inclusive school?
■ What is the purpose of SEN management within an inclusive school?
■ What is Total Quality Management (TQM)? Is this an inclusive model?
■ What is the role of the SENCO within an inclusive school?

Introduction

Effective leadership and management of a school as a learning community is central to the responsibilities of senior leadership (and special educational needs) teams. This chapter provides a guide for school leaders and those having responsibility, such as the school's SENCO and SEN team. The chapter identifies the required systems, structures and roles for the leadership and management of inclusion and SEN in schools. In developing an understanding of the roles of leaders and teachers in relation to learner need, the chapter will provide the reader with guidance on how to create a safe, secure environment for all who experience the learning community. The chapter is presented in four sections:

■ Section One: Defining leadership and management

■ Section Two: Management systems and structures

■ Section Three: The role of the SENCO

■ Section Four: Funding.

Section One: Leadership and management

Since the 1950s, there has been a proliferation of texts on educational management. Many of these texts have been borrowed from commercial and public sector management. In one such text, Blandford (1997) focused on the role of the teachers as managers. The importance of managing the impact of change within education since 1990 has affected the professional lives of all practitioners and managers. Table 5.1 indicates how educational management is now located within a non-hierarchical collegiate setting within this changing context. The flexibility of the practitioner is paramount; collective management is central to good practice.

Table 5.1 The changing culture of schools

From:	To:
Fixed roles	Flexible roles
Individual responsibility	Shared responsibility
Autocratic	Collaborative
Control	Release
Power	Empowerment

John Harvey-Jones, former ICI chairman, compared leaders to conductors of symphony orchestras. A conductor is responsible for interpreting the work of others (composer) through a large body of people (the orchestra) who are divided into teams (instrumental sections) with their own team leaders (principal players). The conductor directs and guides her/his players in order to achieve and communicate (through performances) excellence to a diverse and critical audience. Thus harmony is achieved where dissonance and noise could so easily prevail. It is such harmony that unites an inclusive school that integrates SEN practices within its community.

Similarly, a school leader is responsible for interpreting the work of others (government, LEA and other schools) through a large body of people (staff, parents and pupils) who are divided into teams (academic, pastoral, non-teaching and support) with their own team leaders (middle managers) in order to achieve and communicate excellence (through pupil success) to a diverse and informed audience (educationalists, parents, government). Although the analogy of the orchestra director will not be referred to directly, it permeates the definitions of leadership and management described in this chapter. Teaching and leadership are roles adopted simultaneously by all senior practitioners in their working lives. A leader within education is a teacher, a leader/manager and a team member. SENCOs as team members do things, or as managers get others to do things. How this is achieved is dependent on the leadership style adopted. This will be influenced by:

- previous experience of managers and leaders

- previous experience of managing and leading

- personal qualities and characteristics

- the levels of influence from other agencies

- the function or task.

Rather than being prescriptive, practitioners and managers will recognise that individuals will decide on their own leadership style. Each individual's qualities will be identified according to her/his ability to get the job done. White and Lippitt (1983) provide broad summaries of leadership types:

- autocratic   leader makes all decisions

- democratic   team makes all decisions

- *laissez-faire*   team works on their own and leader participates when necessary.

In some situations it would be impossible for a leader not to be autocratic; crises occur and management decisions have to be made. Fortunately such events do not occur regularly in schools. In the majority of situations it is preferable and advisable to adopt a democratic style of management; a *laissez-faire* approach would not be applicable to school leadership. A middle/senior leader needs to be aware of the difference between collegiality (i.e. working with colleagues) and professional autonomy; teachers will be autonomous within their classrooms; however, the management of professionals requires collegiality. It is self-evident that collaboration and teamwork is essential to effective inclusive practices.

In the context of SEN, teachers, managers and support agencies live in a practical world (Harrison, 1995). Each school is self-centred, self-reliant and culturally 'different' from any other school. In contrast, the leadership structure and organisation of the school will be very similar to that of other schools. There are generic responsibilities, which apply to the leadership and subsequent management of all schools. Head teachers need to give a clear sense of direction and transmit high expectations to staff and pupils, while involving all members of the school community in learning and teaching through:

- clarity of expectations

- creating an atmosphere conducive to effective learning

- a combination of firmness and kindness, together with the expectation of courtesy

- warmth and humour in relationships

- support which helps to combat the problems of a difficult environment

- a general demonstration of sensitivity.

In essence, effective leadership in an inclusive school is marked by a non-confrontational style, where decisiveness is combined with the ability to delegate, listen, enthuse, support and unite the team of staff (Rogers, 1996). Head teachers need to be listeners, so that teachers and pupils should feel able to talk to them in confidence. Head teachers should also aim to discuss inclusion and special educational needs periodically with staff, pupils and the wider school community. Leaders should also emphasise the need for every person to keep the school functioning smoothly and to keep morale at a high level.

The continuous professional development of teaching and non-teaching staff is the responsibility of head teachers and their senior managers. Staff should feel able to discuss the development of their knowledge and understanding, skills and abilities (see Chapter 8). As described throughout this book, schools function within a society where the prevailing ideology is one of inclusion. Table 5.2 provides a further guide to the terminology of inclusion and inclusive schools in the context of schools as organisations, adapted from Tilstone et al. (1998, p. 16), which will inform leadership and management practices.

Table 5.2 Definitions of inclusion within schools as organisations (Adapted from Tilstone et al., 1998, p. 16)

- *Being with one another … How we deal with diversity, how we deal with difference (Forest and Pearpont, 1992).*

- *Inclusive Schools are diverse problem-solving organisations with a common mission that emphasises learning for all students (Rouse and Florian, 1996).*

- *Being a full member of an age appropriate class in your school doing the same lessons as the other pupils and it mattering if you are not there.*

- *A set principle which ensures that the student with a disability is viewed as a valued and needed member of the school community in every respect (Uditsky, 1993).*

- *Inclusion can be understood as a move towards extending the scope of ordinary schools so they can include a great diversity of children (Clark et al., 1995).*

- *Inclusive schools deliver a curriculum to students through organisational arrangements that are different from those used in schools that exclude some students from their regular classrooms (Ballard, 1995).*

- *Increasing participation and decreasing exclusion from mainstream social settings.*

- *Inclusion describes the process by which a school attempts to respond to all its pupils as individuals by reconsidering its curricula organisation and provision.*

- *An inclusive school is one which is accepting of all students (Thomas, 1997).*

Leadership and management of SEN

Effective inclusion relies on more than specialist skills and resources. It requires positive attitudes towards children who have difficulties in school, a greater responsiveness to individual needs and, critically, a willingness among all staff to play their part. The leadership of the head teacher is a key factor in making these happen. The National College for School Leadership (NCSL) has revised its National Standards for Head Teachers to ensure that a far greater emphasis is placed on the role of the head teacher in promoting inclusive practice within their school by:

- creating a positive learning environment for children with SEN and disabilities

- ensuring that staff develop the skills and confidence to respond effectively to children's SEN and disabilities

- promoting collaborative working with special and mainstream schools

- building the confidence of parents in the school's ability to meet their child's needs.

The NCSL is also introducing a new SEN module to the Head Teacher Induction Programme, focused on developing new head teachers' skills and knowledge in these areas.

As stated, the traditional hierarchical model of school management has its roots in Weberian theory. Hoy and Miskel (1991, p. 57) identify the following characteristics of Weber's model of bureaucracy:

- division of labour and specialisation of expertise

- treating everyone equally and on the basis of facts not feelings

- hierarchy of authority for control and decision-making

- rules and regulations on the conduct of work

- career structure to progress up the hierarchy.

Many of these characteristics are seen within contemporary education systems, as the majority of schools operate with a hierarchical management model (Mintzberg, 1983; Blandford, 1997). As Elliott et al. (1981, p. 6) comment:

> *Hierarchical accountability facilitates social control over an organisation by a powerful elite at the top of the pyramid. It is indicative of a bureaucratised school organisation and is concerned with achieving the goals of the organisation.*

What has become apparent is that this traditional form of education management is changing. The overall aims of SENCO responsibilities are to implement the revised CoP (DfES, 2001a) and facilitate an inclusive environment. If the SENCO is to become a school-wide facilitator of teachers and advocate of pupils with SEN within a whole-school team, collaboratively sharing in the management of SEN provision, then a change in the management structure is needed. The *ad hoc* model as depicted by Skrtic (1991, p. 171) over a decade ago allows broadening of staff role and innovative thinking with regards to problem resolution:

> *The difference between the two configurations is that, faced with a problem, the adhocery engages in creative effort to find a novel situation; the professional bureaucracy pigeonholes it into a known contingency to which it can apply a standard program. One engages in divergent thinking aimed at innovation; the other in convergent thinking aimed at perfection.*

This *ad hoc* approach entails de-professionalisation within a collaborative context, innovation and multi-disciplinary teams. Skrtic (1991, p. 171) maintained that in order to develop an *ad hoc* approach to education management one must acknowledge that previous school bureaucracies as rational entities no longer apply:

> *... the trend in organizational analysis, as in the social sciences generally, has been away from the traditional foundational notion of one best theory or paradigm for understanding organization. Thus the contemporary discourse in organizational analysis is characterized by theoretical diversity ... and by an anti-foundational methodological orientation.*

Ad hoc bureaucracy is centred on the premise of critical theory where nothing is taken for granted, no single position or role defined rigidly, and therefore allows innovation to the foundation upon which decisions are made (House, 1979). The effect of the *ad hoc* approach results in the creation of multi disciplinary teams, collaboration between teams, and the use of innovation in resolving problems and realising policy aims and objectives. It would appear that these changes have been occurring in schools since the initial CoP (Gibson, 2001a).

Total Quality Management

An alternative model to adhocery or hierarchical leadership that would seem more appropriate to inclusive schools is Total Quality Management (TQM) which is a holistic approach to management that applies to every relationship and process at all levels of an organisation. TQM is value-driven, placing a fundamental significance on values and purpose (Ormston, 1996). It is concerned with managing the interpersonal components and acknowledges the interdependence between an organisation and its environment. Within a TQM organisation, people are trusted to work as professionals, and there is a strong emphasis on teamwork; however, there is a weak emphasis on hierarchy. Critically the organisation sets clear goals which are communicated. As a consequence every member has high expectations of themselves, so that the organisation is 'fit for purpose'.

Within TQM, quality is internalised as a value at the core of all practice. Central to TQM is that the customer or client is defined as the person or group in receipt of a product or service. The organisation only exists for the customer; there is no other purpose. Once the customers' needs are known, systems are established to manage all processes. The emphasis is on prevention of mistakes and poor quality products. The appropriate procedures are defined by those who have the responsibility to implement them within clear organisational guidelines.

There is no single model for TQM organisations. What is important is that the structure should facilitate the task and process. The theoretical structure of a TQM organisation involves a coalition of autonomous teams able to interact directly with the customer and with each other. These are all linked to senior management teams responsible for strategy.

Teams are fundamental to TQM. Members of teams have explicit and shared values while leadership is based on function and need rather than power and status. There is pride in belonging to the team with clear aims and tasks. Critically the team learns and develops by a process of continuous feedback and review. This process is characterised by a high degree of openness and candour. Essentially decisions are shared. Whether TQM would be applicable to a school or team would be dependent on its culture and ethos. The philosophy of TQM suggests that profound cultural changes are needed within schools.

Leadership and school ethos

Having embraced the concept of leadership style, school leaders should aim to create an atmosphere whereby teachers are able to run organised and effective inclusive classrooms in which:

- the abilities of individual pupils are given the opportunity to develop

- teachers can fulfil their proper function as facilitators of learning

- children can acquire the techniques for monitoring and guiding their own behaviour for learning.

The general atmosphere and practices of schools can, and do, make a substantial difference to pupil learning and attitudes. Research (Rutter et al., 1979; Mortimore et al., 1988) has shown that a range of factors influence learning and teaching:

- academic balance

- appropriateness of the curriculum

- environment

- teacher modelling

- whole-school management

- communication systems.

School leaders will need to consider each of the above in relation to their own school. The need to provide a structure as a point of reference for both pupils and teachers is recognised by practitioners and researchers (Jones, 1989). As an inclusive school, those that embrace TQM as their preferred model will create a structure that will facilitate the task of meeting the needs of all pupils and teachers within the learning community.

Section Two: Management systems and structures

School leadership and management needs to be placed within the context of the management and leadership structures that exist at governmental, LEA and school levels. The leadership structure of the school, LEA and support agencies should be known by all members of the school community and displayed as typically shown in Figure 5.1.

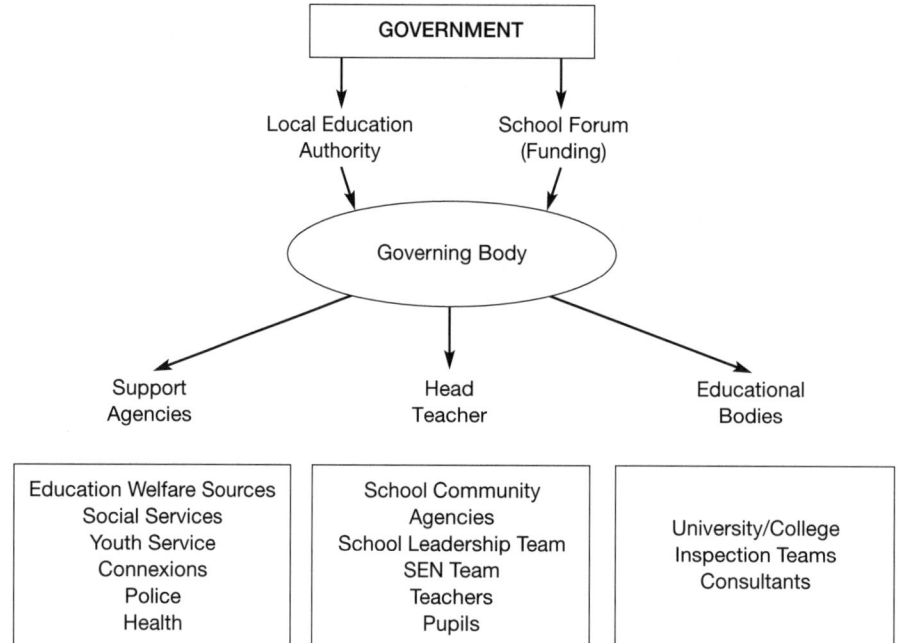

Figure 5.1 School management – external agencies (adapted from Blandford, 1997)

While all managers, leaders and teachers have a responsibility for learning and teaching, a central role of the senior leadership team is the management of staff. In essence, this role should be supportive of the management of the curriculum and resources.

Figure 5.2 reflects the rapid changes that have taken place within the curriculum and the devolution of management responsibilities from LEAs to schools, which have led to a shift in leadership styles. Managers and leaders have to be adaptable; the emphasis is on flexibility, sharing, collaboration and empowerment. SENCOs will be responsible for a team which will have two distinct focuses:

1. Day-to-day management of teaching, learning and resources, collaboration on clearly defined tasks, monitoring and evaluation.

2. Participation by representation in working groups set up by the senior management team to discuss specific tasks or directives from governing agencies or school policy groups.

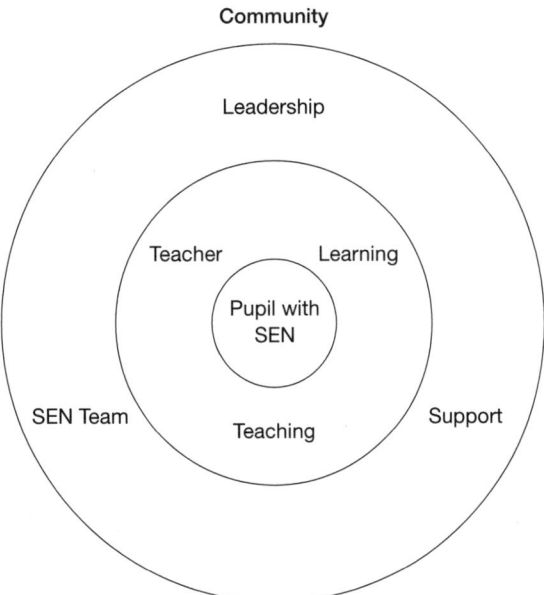

Figure 5.2 Inclusive structure placing the pupil with SEN at the centre

Figure 5.2 also illustrates the importance of the community. Placing the Pupil with SEN at the centre of the figure demonstrates the interrelationship between teachers and leaders in supporting learning and teaching within the school community.

ACTIVITY 5.1: EFFECTIVE MANAGEMENT

How does your school facilitate effective leadership and management with the following members of the school community?

- pupils

- teachers/senior managers

- general assistants/school meal service assistants

- parents

- non-teaching support staff

- governors

- support agencies

- education welfare officers/education officers/children's officers

- support teams/social services

- LEA advisory service

▶

■ educational psychologists

■ youth organisations

■ Connexions

■ medical teams

■ judicial system

■ police.

This page can be photocopied. © *Managing Special Educational Needs*, Gibson and Blandford, 2005

Section Three: The role of the SENCO

Following the initial CoP (DfE, 1994a), the government recognised the need to develop standards for SENCOs in schools. In 1996 the DfEE produced a pamphlet entitled *The Senco Guide* which was followed in 1998 by the Teacher Training Agency (TTA)'s *National Standards for SENCOs,* which provide clarification of their roles and responsibilities.

The standards for SENCOs were revised following wide consultation in England and Wales with teachers, head teachers, professional and subject associations, teacher trainers in schools, LEAs, higher education institutions (HEIs) and SEN organisations. They have also been revised in the light of research undertaken in *The SENCO Guide* (DfEE, 1996). The revised Code of Practice (DfES, 2001a) while addressing some of the main concerns of the SENCO role, is still limited in the detail it provides on how to address these issues.

Table 5.3 summarises the SENCO's responsibilities as indicated in the TTA Standards. Responsibility for inclusive SEN practices resides within and beyond the SEN team. A TQM school will encourage the involvement of all staff in SEN and inclusive practices. Table 5.4 outlines the responsibilities for all members of the school community to assist the SENCO in the management of inclusive and SEN practices.

An unintentional outcome of the CoP (DfE, 1994a; DfES, 2001a) has been that the standards have provided a form of measure that OfSTED could use when inspecting schools and assessing SENCO abilities. Although OfSTED (2004a) recognise the complexities, research indicates that many SENCOs have found themselves heavily burdened with tasks for which they feel untrained and ill-prepared (see Table 2.4).

Table 5.3 Extracts taken from *National Standards for SENCOs* (TTA, 1998, pp. 5–14)

Core purpose of the SENCO	The SENCO takes responsibility for the day-to-day operation of provision made by the school for pupils with SEN and provides professional guidance in the area of SEN in order to secure high quality teaching and the effective use of resources to bring about improved standards of achievement for all pupils.
Key outcomes of SEN co-ordination	a) Pupils on the SEN register make progress. b) Teachers become familiar with, and implement, the school's SEN policy. c) TAs understand their role with respect to pupils with SEN. d) Parents understand the targets set for their children. e) Governors understand their role in relation to pupils with SEN. f) LEA and other responsible bodies receive timely information about the progress made by pupils with SEN.
Professional knowledge and understanding	SENCOs develop the particular aspects of knowledge and understanding required for co-ordinating SEN in a school.
Skills and attributes	SENCOs will be skilled teachers in their right. The head teacher should ensure that the SENCO (if not head teacher) has access to specific training related to the development of these necessary skills: a) Leadership skills attributes and professional competence. b) Decision-making skills. c) Communication skills. d) Self-management.
Key areas of SEN co-ordination	a) Strategic development of SEN provision in school. b) Teaching and learning. c) Leading and managing staff. d) Efficient and effective deployment of staff and resources.

Table 5.4 School staff responsibilities for pupils with SEN (DfES, 2001a, 1: 15)

Member of staff	Responsibilities to pupils with SEN
Governing Body	In co-operation with the head teacher, determines the school's general policy and approach to provision for children with SEN.
Governing Body Learning and Teaching Committee	To take particular interest in and closely monitor the school's work on behalf of children with SEN.
Head teacher	Responsibility for the day-to-day management of the provision for children with SEN. The head teacher will work closely with the school SENCO and SEN team as well as keep governors informed.
Classroom teacher	All teachers to be fully aware of their part in providing for pupils with SEN, e.g. effective differentiation of lessons as well as be involved in the development of the school's SEN policy.
SENCO and SEN team	Working closely with the whole-school community to determine the strategic development of the SEN policy and provision as well as having responsibility for the day-to-day operation of the school's SEN policy and for co-ordinating provision for pupils with SEN.

Funding a full-time SENCO for every 500 pupils could become the standard provision of local authorities following DfES guidance on the management of expenditure to meet special educational needs (DfES, 2004c). On delegating resources to mainstream settings, the document recommends that local authorities identify an amount within the per pupil allocation to support the cost of SENCO duties and responsibilities.

The guidance makes clear that the cost of SENCO time should come from the school's base budget and not from the additional resources allocated for SEN. It notes that some LEAs have identified an amount within the Age Weighted Pupil Unit (AWPU) allocation to meet the cost of SENCO time. For example, the average cost of employing a SENCO is identified and included within the AWPU at a rate sufficient to provide at least one full-time equivalent member of staff per 500 pupils.

SENCOs are player managers, participating in the daily tasks of teaching while fulfilling the role of a team leader. As a player manager, they need to know the role of a senior leader or middle leader in relation to both leaders and the team. A middle leader is led by a senior leadership team, the governing body and her/his line manager. There is a likelihood that a SENCO will join teams with responsibility for the management of the school. It is essential therefore for SENCOs to:

- know their role
- know their team
- know their managers.

A team leader has to be able to work in an open and honest manner. As professionals, teachers should value effective teamwork on which schools depend. The characteristics of effective teams are (Hall and Oldroyd, 1990; Coleman and Bush, 1994):

- *Clear objectives and goals* – *according to task.*

- *Openness and confrontation* – *dependent on effective communication and interpersonal relationships.*

- *Support and trust* – *requiring active listening and understanding.*

- *Co-operation and conflict* – *working together, sharing and developing ideas in a democratic and creative manner.*

- *Sound procedures* – *enable everyone to contribute to decision-making.*

- *Appropriate leadership* – *knowing and understanding team members, their beliefs and values.*

- *Regular review* – *monitoring and evaluating in a rigorous manner.*

- *Individual development* – *enabling individuals to develop strengths, involving appraisal and staff development.*

- *Sound inter-group relations* – *a commitment to teaching pupils through openness and trust.*

The development of teams is critical to effective inclusion. Many schools pay lip-service to the idea of team management. Activity 5.2 might prove to be a useful exercise in the development of inclusive SEN teams.

ACTIVITY 5.2: DEVELOPING TEAMS

The following exercise can be used with a SEN team. This exercise could form part of an INSET day or an evening (twilight) session. The exercise could be facilitated by a senior member of staff or middle manager with team-building experience.

SEN team development plan

Aims: To examine SEN team aims

To examine teaching and learning styles/differentiation

To identify areas of weakness in resourcing.

Time: 1 hour

Stage 1 (5 minutes)

Brainstorm the context that you are working in. Consider all factors inside and beyond the school and write these up on a flipchart.

Stage 2 (15 minutes)

Divide into two groups. Look at the school SEN aims. How do the SEN department/team aims reflect those of the school? Write on a flipchart what the aims should be – how can you implement these aims?

Stage 3 (10 minutes)

Share your ideas with the SEN team.

Stage 4 (10 minutes)

Working individually, describe how you organise your teaching/tasks. Compare notes with a colleague.

Stage 5 (20 minutes)

Discuss successful strategies for raising achievement through planning/completing tasks/teaching and learning styles. List, ready for presentation.

This page can be photocopied. © *Managing Special Educational Needs*, Gibson and Blandford, 2005

Effective communication

SEN leaders will communicate with colleagues, parents, pupils and other agencies; therefore communication is central to effective school operations. According to Hoy and Miskel (1991):

> *communication underlies all organisational and administrative situations, and is essential to decision-making and effective leadership ... At the heart of communication lies the opportunity to resolve contradictions, quell rumours, provide reassurance, and, ultimately, instil meaning in the complex but engaging task of education.*

In schools, practitioners and managers use different methods of communication for different purposes. Why is it that communication always seems to flow more smoothly in some schools, teams and departments than in others? One reason is the established communication climate. The conditions in which ideas, information and feelings are exchanged directly influence the extent to which communication is a positive or negative force in a school. A supportive communication climate promotes co-operative working relationships, leading to effective information gathering and transfer. Supportiveness is communicated most clearly by the following kinds of responses (NPBEA, 1993, 16:4):

Descriptive	*statements are informative not evaluative.*
Solution-orientated	*there is a focus on problem-solving rather than on what cannot be done.*
Open and honest	*even if criticism is expressed, there are rarely hidden messages; the aim is to help and improve.*
Caring	*emphasis on empathy and understanding.*
Egalitarian	*communications value everyone, regardless of their role or status.*
Forgiving	*error is recognised and minimised.*
Feedback	*a positive and essential part of maintaining good working relationships and high levels of performance.*

In an open and supportive communication climate, staff feel valued, crises are dealt with and staff are more open themselves. They will feel trusted, secure and confident in their jobs and in the organisation as a whole. Effective team-working, flexibility and a sense of involvement all contribute to, and benefit from, an open and supportive climate.

The closed communication climate is the antithesis of the above. Where the environment is highly political, competition for approval, promotion or resources is high on the hidden agenda. Control is often maintained through the suppression of open forms of communication. Communication behaviours that are likely to predominate in a closed communication environment include the following (NPBEA, 1993, 16:4):

Judgemental	*emphasis on apportioning blame; feedback is negative; people feel inferior.*
Controlling	*people are expected to conform to certain types of behaviour.*
Deceptive	*messages are manipulative and hold hidden meaning.*
Non-caring	*communication is detached, impersonal with little concern for others.*
Superior	*interaction emphasises differences in status, skills and understanding.*
Dogmatic	*little discussion; unwillingness to accept other points of view.*
Hostile	*a predominantly negative approach, placing little importance on the needs of others.*

A closed climate may be a direct outcome of management style. As a middle manager, you will need to encourage an open and positive climate within your team or department. Some methods of communication may be more effective than others, depending on the situation. Communication is the exchange of information, which can range from an informal discussion with a colleague to a full report to school governors. Channels of communications in school can be summarised as follows:

Communication channel	Descriptors
Oral – spoken word	most preferred – direct and personal.
Written	letters, memos, reports, e-mail; therefore consistent and available for future reference.
Meetings	two or more people, formal/informal, planned/unplanned, structured/unstructured.
Telephone calls	Immediate, time consuming, a degree of personal contact.

There are advantages and disadvantages to each channel of communication, which are not mutually exclusive. Meetings may fulfil social needs as well as more formal requirements. In addition to the above, schools may have briefings, newsletters (information sheets), notice boards, prospectuses and informal conversations (chats). Any passing of information between two people will involve communication.

The aims of communication also focus on seeking information, instructing, motivating, encouraging, supporting and persuading (Hall and Oldroyd, 1990). As a manager you will need to decide on the purpose of your communication – the message and the most effective means of communicating. An understanding of the communication process will produce effective results (NPBEA, 1993, 16:19). The communication process involves:

1. Message — can be intended or unintended; needs to be clear.

2. Encoding — the ability to put thoughts or words into actions.

3. Setting — as appropriate – classroom, boardroom, conference room, office.

4. Transmission — to communicate effectively, messages must be well organised, clear and must make appropriate use of words and body language.

5. Decoding — the process of interpreting messages.

6. Message received — this may happen simultaneously to the giving of the message.

7. Feedback — as a message is decoded the receiver responds to it; listening is critical.

Some people appear to have an innate ability to communicate; many others acquire skills through study and practice. Potential barriers to communicating; according to NPBEA (1993, 16:13), are:

1. Filtering of information – not telling the 'whole story'.

2. Organisational structure – inappropriate administration.

3. Information overload – inappropriate timing and content.

4. Semantics – different words have different meanings.

5. Status differences – status/roles can interfere with the meaning of the message.

6. Over interpretation – reading too much into the message.

7. Evaluative tendencies – qualitative judgements.

8. Stereotypes – negative stereotypes based on race, sex, age, role, etc.

9. Cultural and gender differences.

10. Arrogance and Superiority.

Written communication

SEN leaders in schools require the ability to communicate clearly in writing. There will be occasions when you will use both spoken and written communication in order to convey a message. As leaders and role models, managers are in a position to improve communication by their quality of writing as well as by providing an example to teachers and students. Managers also have an impact on student education, teacher outlook and school image (NPBEA, 1993, 17:5). There is a strong relationship between written skills and job effectiveness.

Identification of audience is important for all forms of communication. Before writing, you need to consider your audience, to be clear what it is you are trying to communicate, and feel confident that you have the writing skills necessary to convey your message to your intended audience. The process of writing will also be dependent on the purpose. A memo to a colleague, for example, will not involve the same amount of detailed preparation as a report for the senior management team or governors. It is essential that SEN leaders identify their audience in order to adopt the appropriate style of written communication.

The tools of written communication are sound grammar, accurate spelling, structure and punctuation. Each sentence will need to be effective, forming part of the message. The NPBEA (1993, 17:14) suggests the following stages of the writing process:

1. Pre-writing

2. Drafting

3. Revising

4. Editing

5. Final Product.

For documents to be read in detail, they should be easy to read and visually appealing. The choice of format will enhance the document's message. The presentation of the text should do justice to its content. The following are key features for effective presentation:

1. Clear title which identifies the content and meaning of the text

2. Appropriate headings and subheadings

3. Visual impact – do not overcrowd each page

4. Double space

5. Use a simple type font (size 12)

6. Use numbering when necessary (titles, paragraphs, pages)

7. Summarise key points by using lists

8. Label as appropriate

9. Use capitals, bold, underlining and italics

10. Longer documents should have:

    – contents table

    – introduction

    – summary

    – index

    – appendix

11. Binding – use an attractive folder and/or cover.

SEN leaders should ensure that team members follow good practice when preparing written documents. Development of 'house-style' would enhance the effectiveness of a school's/team's communication with its audience.

Meetings

A significant difference to a teacher newly appointed as a SENCO is the importance of meetings. The number of meetings held in a school will reflect the size and culture of the school. Whatever the number of meetings, practitioners and managers often have the impression that meetings are a waste of time. Before planning a meeting it would be useful to reflect whether a meeting is necessary. The advantages and disadvantages of meetings should be considered:

Advantages

- communication
- improve staff skills in communication and decision-making
- sense of involvement and ownership among staff
- democratic – improve job satisfaction
- keep managers and staff in touch.

Disadvantages

- time – meetings take longer to reach decisions and take teachers away from preparation, marking and contact with pupils
- expense – is this the best use of non-contact time?
- limited control – can be dominated by the most senior or the most vocal
- decision-making and communication dependent on the quality of the meeting.

If the quality of school meetings is to improve, it is necessary for all staff to understand the function of each meeting. SEN leaders are required to plan, lead and participate in meetings which may have one or more of the following functions:

- to communicate information – giving and receiving
- to take decisions
- to influence (and understand) policy
- to monitor and evaluate
- to problem solve
- to plan
- to develop co-operation and commitment
- to motivate.

As stated earlier, the size and culture of the school will determine the number of meetings held. Similarly the culture and style of each meeting will determine its effectiveness. Understanding the culture and style of meetings will help teachers and managers to:

- make better use of the opportunities
- alter the culture and style, when appropriate.

Meetings develop according to the membership of the team or group, sometimes producing a change in culture and style; this may need to be part of more radical changes in the school as a whole. There are usually two key roles in formal meetings: chair and secretary (minute taker) (Hedge et al., 1994, pp. 42–62). SEN leaders may be required to chair team meetings and act as secretary to senior management or staff meetings. It is not advisable to chair and take minutes simultaneously. The collective functions of the chair and secretary are:

1. to progress the meeting efficiently

2. to maintain the meeting as a viable working group.

In addition, chairs will decide whether a meeting is to be formal or informal, generally dependent on the function and/or purpose of the meeting. A chair or secretary will then proceed as follows:

Before the meeting

■ prepare an agenda in advance of the meeting to allow members to consider each point and allow other points to be added to the agenda

■ distribute the necessary papers.

During the meeting

■ open the meeting

■ state the purpose of the meeting

■ take the meeting through the agenda

■ close the meeting

■ ensure fair play

■ stay in charge

■ control length and depth of discussions

■ summarise discussion

■ end discussion

■ ensure decisions are taken appropriately, i.e. conduct a vote, check consensus

■ encourage participation.

After the meeting

- pursue discussions/actions

- represent the team at other meetings.

When preparing to chair a meeting, a middle manager should:

- read the necessary papers

- obtain briefing from colleagues, when required

- think through the process (mentally rehearse each item)

- anticipate conflict

- contact speakers/participants to ensure that they are aware of when (and for how long) they are required to speak

- check procedures and rules – know to whom the meeting should report.

Effective chairing of meetings will require effective interpersonal skills. It is the chair's responsibility to ensure that the atmosphere of the meeting is conducive to discussion and that members feel valued. SEN leaders need to develop skills in managing teams during meetings. Take the lead, talk to people, establish acceptable behaviour and set a good example. Haynes (1988, pp. 62–5) suggested that if conflict arises, it can be dealt with by:

- Clarifying objectives

- Striving for understanding

- Focusing on the rational

- Generating alternatives

- Postponing the issue

- Using humour.

A chair with a sense of humour may be able to diffuse the situation. Detailed planning may also avoid possible areas/items of conflict. Problems will arise if meetings have unclear objectives and lack leadership. Avoid holding meetings with large groups of people. Have a clear agenda and keep to time.

SEN leaders will be required to participate in meetings. Aim to become a valued member. The hardest part of managing meetings is arriving at group decisions. This will be discussed later. In sum, a group consensus can be reached if appropriate behaviour is practised in meetings. It is essential for chairs and secretaries to evaluate their practice and to change it if required. With good leadership, meetings can be effective.

Notice boards/displays

SEN leaders will have notice boards which are used to communicate with parents, pupils and colleagues. Schools are often visited by members of the public and outside agencies in addition to their own clientele. It is therefore necessary for staff to consider the following:

1. Who will see the message?

2. Who is the message for?

3. What will be communicated by the quality of the message/display and its presentation?

4. How involved are the pupils?

5. Should parents/pupils/other agencies read the message – what other means are there to communicate the message?

6. Is there a 'house-style' that should be adopted?

Section Four: Funding

One aspect of education management and leadership not covered in full in this book is that of funding and financial management. Given the complexities of funding and recurring changes, the authors recommend that managers and leaders engage in further reading. The following extract from SENCO Update, September 2004, provides further guidance on *The Management of SEN Expenditure* (DfES, 2004c).

> *The management of SEN expenditure aims to provide information and suggested approaches for local authorities that are finding it difficult to manage SEN expenditure. The Department is recruiting a number of SEN expert authorities to provide additional support and challenge. Management of SEN resources will be a priority for the new service.*

Delegating resources to mainstream settings

The document recommends that local authorities:

- *delegate SEN resources to mainstream schools*

- *develop a funding formula to allocate resources for most pupils with additional and special educational needs*

- *develop arrangements to distribute additional resources for pupils with the most severe and complex SEN*

- *work with schools and other stakeholders to ensure that respective responsibilities are clear and to build parental confidence*

- *ensure that the required provision can be delivered, particularly where statements are maintained.*

Managing change

Changing the way in which SEN resources are distributed takes time, typically 12 months. The guidance offers a sample timetable for LEAs implementing change over this period involving the following steps:

- *Form a project group or use an existing forum of key stakeholders including:*

  - *Schools (head teachers, SENCOs and governors) – nominated by local associations; include all phases of education and types of schools*

  - *Parents – nominations from voluntary organisations that represent parents, obtained through the parent partnership services*

  - *Health and children's social services*

  - *LEA officers leading on SEN, school improvement and finance*

  - *Other representatives, including early years and Connexions.*

- *Identify and benchmark current expenditure with a number of similar authorities – reducing expenditure lines to costs per pupil. Much expenditure on SEN and inclusion in mainstream settings may be hidden within the Individual Schools Budget (ISB).*

- *Identify the principles with the project group to underpin the new resource strategy.*

- *Consult widely on these principles with schools and other stakeholders.*

- *Consider the outcomes of the consultation with the project group.*

- *Identify the preferred way forward, including any proposed changes to local Fair Funding arrangements.*

- *Model the impact of the proposed changes on a school by school basis, showing comparisons between existing and proposed resource allocations. Modelling will probably have to be refined several times.*

- *Consider any transitional arrangements that might be required and model these.*

- *Draft formal consultation papers and discuss these with both the project group and the members of the schools forum.*

● *Carry out formal consultation together with open meetings of head teachers, governors, SENCOs, parents and voluntary organisations.*

● *Consider the outcomes of the consultation and report these to the project group, elected members and the schools forum. Make any necessary changes to proposals and arrangements for the implementation from elected members and the schools forum.*

● *Support implementation with straightforward information, advice and briefing sessions for head teachers, SENCOs, parents and governors. Ensure that all materials comply with the Special Educational Needs (Provision of Information by LEAs) (England) Regulations 2001. These are reproduced at the back of the SEN Code of Practice.*

The guidance also offers advice on SEN expenditure in special schools, early years settings and post-16 provision.

Executive summary

■ Schools function within a society where the prevailing ideology is one of inclusion.

■ Effective management and leadership of the school as a learning community is central to the role and responsibilities of senior leadership teams and head teachers.

■ Having embraced the concept of style, school leaders should aim to create an atmosphere whereby teachers are able to run organised and effective classrooms.

■ The general atmosphere and practices of schools can make a substantial difference to pupil learning and attitudes.

■ SENCOs are player managers, participating in the daily tasks of teaching while fulfilling the role of team leader.

■ The working context for the role of the SENCO in primary and secondary schools is the revised Code of Practice for Special Educational Needs.

■ An unintentional outcome of the standards was that they were used to provide a form of measure that OfSTED would use when inspecting schools and assessing SENCO abilities.

■ The opportunity to participate in decision-making teams which impact on school management is a relatively new phenomenon.

■ Management and leadership require effective communication systems.

■ Funding for SEN requires planning, budgeting and careful management.

Further reading

Blandford, S. (1997), *Middle Management in Schools*, London: Pitman

Blandford, S. and Blackburn, N. (2004), *School Financial Management Handbook*, London: Optimus

Caldwell, B.J. and Spinks, J.M. (1998), *Beyond the Self-Managing School*, London: Falmer Press

Jones, N. (ed.) (1989), *School Management and Pupil Behaviour*, Lewes: Falmer Press

Katz, D. and Kahn, R.L. (1978,) *The Social Psychology of Organizations*, New York: John Wiley

Mintzberg, H. (1983), *Power in and around Organizations*, New Jersey: Prentice-Hall

External Agencies and the School Community

CHAPTER 6: KEY QUESTIONS TO BE CONSIDERED
■ What are the principles that underpin collaborative, multi-agency practice in schools?
■ What are the responsibilities of the LEA and support agencies?
■ What is the purpose of Individual Action Plans?
■ How can Individual Action Plans be embedded within curriculum and learning and teaching strategies in your school?
■ What are the staff development needs associated with effective collaborative multi-agency practice?

Introduction

This chapter provides guidance on the roles and responsibilities of professional agencies involved in the management of SEN in school. Specifically, the relationship of the SENCO to LEA support services, health, social services and other agencies within the community will be examined. Examples will be given including a case study involving an educational psychologist working with a unitary authority with very specific environmental needs. The chapter is presented in four sections:

■ Section One defines the principles underpinning good practice in working with a range of agencies in support of pupils with SEN.

■ Section Two describes a selection of government agencies who work in partnership with schools. There are also a number of independent consultants and agents who provide additional expertise.

■ Section Three provides guidance on preparing educational plans for pupils with SEN. Advice is also given on how to review educational plans.

■ Section Four presents a case study highlighting effective partnership in practice.

The need for multi-agency consultation and communication in support of pupils with SEN is self-evident. The level of consultation that actually happens is dependent on the relationship between the school, each agency within the LEA and external agents, as well as on the communication skills of those involved. It is evident that teachers and school leadership teams need to develop a comprehensive understanding of the role of each agency in relation to pupils with SEN.

Following the 1988 Education Reform Act, many LEA agencies were reorganised as a direct response to the devolution of resource management under the Local Management of Schools (LMS). LEAs are currently responsible for the provision of four general kinds of service to schools; each relevant to the management of inclusion and SEN:

- co-ordinating the introduction of national initiatives

- providing a range of personnel services including professional advice to governors

- providing client-based services for individual pupils, parents and teachers

- long-term planning of educational provision.

LEAs are responsible for funding support agencies including education welfare officers (EWOs), support teachers for pupils experiencing Behavioural, Emotional and Social Difficulties (BESD), and educational psychologists. Schools are responsible for contributing funds to BESD pupils, TAs, the remodelled workforce and lunchtime supervisors. Schools are also responsible for establishing and maintaining home–school contracts as a means of improving communication and teacher–parent relationships. The wealth of support available to pupils and teachers for support of pupils with SEN is a significant reflection of the need for schools to provide a safe, secure and inclusive environment for all members of the school community. Practice is often determined by the values and principles held by the senior leadership team.

Section One: Principles

Meeting the special educational needs of individual pupils requires flexible working of statutory agencies. SENCOs and staff should communicate and agree policies and protocols which ensure that there is a seamless service. Working supportively, and in partnership with parents and pupils, will ensure that everyone involved understands the responses of the professionals concerned, and lead to a better quality, more meaningful provision. Maintained schools must publish information on the school's arrangements for working in partnership with LEA support services, health and social services, the Connexions service and any relevant local and national voluntary organisations. It should be recognised that external support services can play an important part in helping schools identify, assess and make provision for pupils with SEN. It is self-evident that all services for pupils with SEN should focus on identifying and addressing the needs of children and enabling them to improve their situation through:

- early identification

- continual engagement with the child and parents

- focused intervention

- dissemination of effective approaches and techniques.

The objective is to provide an integrated, high quality, holistic support that focuses on the needs of the child. Such provision should be based on a shared perspective and should build on mutual understanding and agreement where all voices are heard. Services should adopt a flexible pupil-centred approach to service delivery to ensure that the changing needs and priorities of the child and her/his parents can be met at any given time.

All agencies will need to recognise the need for effective collaboration of services involved with the pupil and parents. Consultative responsibilities and effective communication systems at management and practitioner levels will then be clearly identified. Developments in organisational structures and working practices will need to reflect this principle. Joint planning arrangements would then:

- take account of good practice

- ensure consultation with all relevant services

- agree priorities

- publicise decisions to parents and professionals

- regularly review policies and objectives.

Local Education Authority (LEA)

Practice within LEAs is varied and experience has shown that several have complex support structures that remain unknown or unclear in practice to practitioners in schools. Central to the effectiveness of LEA support teams and other support agencies is their ability to communicate their role to classroom teachers. Often the point of contact in schools is the SENCO. Procedures will need to be developed if teachers are to receive support from other agencies in the education of pupils with SEN.

In practice, all teachers need to have knowledge and understanding of the Code of Practice as it is the framework for recognising and managing pupils with SEN. Rather than leaving the SENCO to deal with all pupils with SEN, all teachers should consider their responsibilities to pupils in their classrooms. LEA support services can provide advice to practitioners, e.g. on teaching techniques and strategies, classroom management, and curriculum materials as well as:

- support for curriculum development

- direct teaching or practical support for class teachers

- part-time specialist help

- access to learning support assistance.

Such services include: specialist teachers of pupils with hearing, visual and speech and language impairments; teachers providing more general learning and behaviour support services; counsellors and educational psychologists; and advisers or teachers of pupils with SEN. Curriculum support and advisory services can also be a resource for advice on specific subject-related learning and teaching techniques and strategies for preparing differentiated and appropriate curriculum materials.

As stated, LEAs should provide full information to all schools about the range of locally available services and how they can be secured. The SENCO and senior leadership team should be aware of the LEA's policy for the provision of support services and how the school can access them. Whether or not funding for particular support services is delegated to schools, it may be helpful for schools and LEAs to draw up agreements for such services, specifying the scope, quality and duration of the service to be provided. When schools enter into contracts with private or voluntary sector providers, they should also satisfy themselves of the qualifications and experience of the specialists involved and that the service represents good value for money, and carry out appropriate police checks.

It is most likely that schools will consult specialists when they take action on behalf of a child through *School Action Plus* (DfES, 2001b). Nevertheless, the involvement of specialists need not be limited to children receiving provision through *School Action Plus*. Outside specialists can play an important part in the very early identification of SEN and in advising schools on effective provision designed to prevent the development of more significant needs. They can also act as consultants and be a source for in-service advice on learning, teaching, behaviour management and specialist strategies for all teachers.

KEY QUESTIONS

- How does your school engage with external agencies?

- Is there a school policy on identifying support for pupils?

- How involved are parents in determining support for their child?

- Does the LEA provide adequate information on the support services available for pupils with SEN?

- What are the school's staff development needs?

ACTIVITY 6.1: PUPIL SUPPORT

Consider how evident the following are in the support you provide for pupils. The direct support to pupils will be managed in a range of ways by:

- gathering information from pupil, school, home, community, other agencies

- assessing the pupil by identifying patterns

- understanding and observation

- planning for school, home and the community

- defining intervention procedures, including group work, work in classroom, work off-site, continued observation, a combination of approaches and a watching brief

- reviewing dates planned well in advance, especially those required in the Code of Practice (DfE 1994a; DfES, 2001a).

The range of pupil support includes:

- classroom observation

- lunchtime and break observation

- one-to-one counselling

- social and interpersonal skills group work

- anger management and conflict resolution group work

- friendship groups support work

- lunchtime clubs and playground support

- therapeutic use of art, drama, play and music

- co-operative games

- home–school liaison

- support for parents

- classroom-focused support work

- off-site curriculum-focused work at Child and Family Support Centres (CFSCs)

This page can be photocopied. © *Managing Special Educational Needs*, Gibson and Blandford, 2005

Section Two: Multi-agency support – external agents

Educational psychology service

A highly specialist area of education provision is that of educational psychology service. An educational psychologist (EP) provides psychological support and advice for pupils to schools, parents, the education department, social services, health services and to the pupils themselves. EPs are trained, experienced professionals bound by professional codes of conduct to act in the best interests of the individual pupils referred to them. They work with parents, teachers and other professionals to help pupils succeed, to prevent or minimise difficulties. Their work is concerned with:

- learning, language and literacy

- specific learning difficulties

- behaviour, emotions or social problems

- physical or sensory difficulties.

The role of EPs is central to the assessment and statementing of pupils with SEN. The EP provides an effective consultation, assessment, advice and intervention service for pupils who may have SEN and for other pupils about whom there may be concern. They also provide in-service training and support research projects involving teachers, other professionals and parents in fulfilling their aim to promote a wider understanding of pupils' needs.

In legislative terms, an EP will inform and advise LEA officers regarding the needs of pupils in relation to the 1993 Education Act and the revised CoP (DfES, 2001a). As such, they will be in contact with pupils, parents, head teachers, governors, LEA and social services officers and a wide range of professional and other staff from all agencies providing services to the local community.

In practice, EPs will be assigned a number of nursery, primary and secondary schools. They will consult with the head teacher to establish priorities according to the needs of the pupils in the school. At stages 1 and 2 of the Code of Practice they will consult with the head teacher and class teacher. At stage 3 the EP will also work with pupils and their families to assess, advise and produce action plans for pupils with SEN.

The EP will also provide a range of in-service courses for parents and professionals that focus on:

- pupil needs

- action planning

- individual and whole-school behaviour policies

- mediation and negotiation

- assertive discipline for teachers and parents

- development of teacher self-esteem

- inclusion issues

- special learning difficulties.

The educational psychology team is central to the planning of multi-agency support for pupils and families with SEN. They advise the LEA on the allocation of the funding that will provide schools with teachers and learning support assistants. The level of service will vary according to available funding. Teachers need to know and understand the role of the EP in relation to their school, if pupils are to receive preventative support that is needed.

Behaviour and Educational Support Team

Behaviour and Educational Support Teams (BEST) do far more than their title implies. BEST teachers are specialists who provide a range of services to mainstream school and specialist schools. They are experts in the management of discipline in schools and of those pupils with related SEN. BEST staff are highly qualified professionals able to deal with difficult pupils. They are also able to deal tactfully and effectively with teachers in mainstream schools who need their help, yet may feel defensive about seeking it. Within the BEST team there will be a team leader, specialist teachers, special needs support assistants and administrative support staff, and the team, which can be set up to provide a service to schools to support pupils experiencing BESD in their mainstream setting and help maintain their places in mainstream education and to access the National Curriculum by:

- providing direct support to individual pupils

- providing practical advice on support strategies to staff

- working with parents/guardians to support their child's educational needs

- assisting schools in developing their own support structures and expertise

- working with social services, health and other education agencies to encourage continuity of support and exchange of information.

In the majority of LEAs, pupils may be referred for BEST support with or without a Statement of Special Educational Needs. Support for non-statemented pupils can be obtained when the pupil's school placement has broken down. Referrals will also require evidence that the pupil still exhibits inappropriate behaviour after receiving support from the school.

Child and Family Support Centre (CFSC)

The aim of CFSCs is to modify the demands made by a pupil or her/his school. These demands are understood to relate to the pressures on the pupil, from home and community, and the developmental needs of the child which relate to her/his previous life experiences. The centres may encourage the school to modify its demands on the pupil. This necessitates the school being well informed about the individual circumstances of the child within the family setting. The underlying principle to the CFSC approach is based on the notion that a pupil's development and self-concept is primarily formed by her/his family and educational experience.

Education Welfare Officer (EWO)

Schools may expect the EWO to undertake many core functions such as attendance, exclusion, child protection, welfare benefits, but also to have duties relating to SEN where the EWO has had direct involvement with the pupil, to support parents and pupils in the process of formal assessment.

EWOs can also advise and support schools in relation to general welfare issues affecting pupils, which can include breakdown in communication between school and home, under-achievement which could be caused by a domestic problem and/or the child not being properly cared for at home.

The Education Welfare Service (EWS) in the majority of LEAs are active in their consultation with other agencies within the authority, including social services, medical and legal services. The complexity of other LEA support agencies is such that a detailed description of each agency would not be appropriate in the context of this book. However, teachers and school managers should be aware of the existence and status of such agencies in relation to pupils with SEN.

Health services

Health Authorities and LEAs must comply with a request from a social services department (SSD) for assistance in providing services for children in need, so long as the request is compatible with their duties and does not unduly prejudice the discharge of any of their functions.

Health Authorities must comply with a request for help from an LEA in connection with children with SEN, unless they consider that the help is not necessary for the exercise of the LEA's functions.

A school's first point of contact with health services will be through the local school health services, which deliver health advisory and support services to schools. These health professionals will usually be able to advise the school, but should also advise the medical officer designated to work with children with SEN that the school has sought advice about a child. Health professionals such as speech and language therapists, occupational therapists and physiotherapists, as well as doctors and the school nurse, also provide advice and support for children with SEN (for further details, see Chapter 4).

The Connexions service

The LEA must have in place arrangements for working with Connexions to ensure the needs of all young people between the ages of 13 and 19 are fully served. The Connexions service provides guidance and support to young people through their teenage years and into adult life. The service is delivered primarily through a network of personal advisers linked with specialist support services. The personal advisers are supported by a comprehensive and coherent service.

The service gives priority to those young people at greatest risk of not making a successful transition to adulthood. The service will have a particular role to play in ensuring the participation and progression of young people with SEN. The service has a key role in the transition process for young people with SEN from Year 9 onwards. Exceptionally, a person with complex learning difficulties or disabilities may need continued enhanced guidance beyond the age of 19. The level of support should be agreed and reviewed jointly by the Connexions service and the local Learning and Skills Council (LSC) and agreement reached as to who will be responsible for the provision of information, advice and guidance.

Social Services

Schools should be aware of the range of local services provided by social services departments (SSDs). SSDs have duties under the 1989 Children Act to provide a range of services for children regarded as being in need. The designated teacher for 'looked after children' should work closely with the SENCO when the pupil also has special educational needs. Schools should also ensure that, where a child is 'looked after' by the local authority, that the child's social worker, and where possible, the parents are involved in their child's education and all processes relating to SEN.

The voluntary sector

Voluntary agencies and groups have an important role to play in meeting the needs of pupils with SEN. They provide services and in some cases offer their own provision. It is essential that LEAs, schools and local authorities seek to work actively in partnership with the voluntary sector to meet pupils' needs. LEAs and schools should demonstrate a willingness to work with and value the contribution. Local authorities also need to help join up the different local partners in order to maximise the benefit for pupils.

Regional partnerships

The DfES sponsors a network of eleven SEN regional partnerships. These partnerships bring together groups of local authorities and local health, social services, voluntary and private sector partners. The overall aim of the network is to secure greater consistency in the quality of the response to pupils with similar SEN.

KEY QUESTIONS
■ What are the systems for engaging multi-agency support in your school?
■ How are staff informed of the support provided for pupils they teach?
■ Is multi-agency support recorded, monitored, reviewed and evaluated?
■ What is the role of the SEN team in managing multi-agency support?

ACTIVITY 6.2: EXTERNAL AGENCIES CONTACT LIST

List the external agencies working in partnership with your school related to the provision of children with SEN.

List contact names, e-mails and phone numbers, and point of contact within your school.

External agency	Name	E-mail	Phone number	School contact

Section Three: Individual Education Plans

The revised CoP (DfES, 2001a) advises that all statemented pupils, i.e. those with SEN, should have an Individual Education Plan (IEP). This is a plan of action focusing on individual pupil needs following a period of consultation with all relevant agencies. A multi-agency report will set the parameters for the IEP. The plan will identify targets and strategies for each pupil and her/his teachers to focus on achieving success.

Set within the context of *School Action Plus* (DfES, 2001b), IEPs provide teachers and support agencies with a joint framework for supporting a pupil with SEN. In consultation with the pupil and parents/guardians, the SENCO and class teacher should decide on the action needed to help the pupil to progress in the light of her/his earlier assessment. One approach might be to provide different learning materials or special equipment; to introduce some group or individual support; to devote extra adult time to devising the nature of the planned intervention and monitoring its effectiveness; or to undertake staff development and training to introduce more effective strategies. Speedy access to LEA support services for one-off or occasional advice on strategies or equipment or for staff training may make it possible to provide effective intervention without the need for regular or ongoing input from external agencies.

IEPs are a useful mechanism for evaluating the needs of each pupil with learning or behavioural problems. EPs, EWOs, EBD support teachers and education officers value the inclusion of IEPs in school SEN policies. Senior leaders and SEN teams will need to provide teachers and support staff with guidance in preparing and implementing an IEP.

ACTIVITY 6.3: STEPS IN PREPARING AN INDIVIDUAL EDUCATION PLAN

Assess the following steps against your own practice.

- Identify the problem, individual teacher or team
- Identify pupil and teacher needs
- Negotiate a feasible strategy, agreed by a team of practitioners
- Create a time-scale for action
- Determine desired outcomes and evaluate actual outcomes
- Monitor progress.

This page can be photocopied. © *Managing Special Educational Needs*, Gibson and Blandford, 2005

Education planning should be supported and enhanced by clear record-keeping systems. The process should formalise specific behaviour/learning targets and provide a written basis for action. As a pupil-centred mechanism, plans must consider:

- feelings of all involved
- strengths and weaknesses of all involved

- areas to develop

- what must be done

- who should do it

- when it should be done by.

Critically, all targets must be positive and meaningful. Once agreed, the education plan must be resourced in order to achieve the set targets. The three main areas of resourcing are people, time and materials/equipment. The management of resources must be established if adequate support is to be given.

ACTIVITY 6.4: SMART PRACTICE

Education planning is based on the principle of an agreement entered into by all involved. As with all plans, the targets set within an action plan will need to be:

Specific   –   clearly stated

Measurable   –   all must agree on how success will be assessed

Attainable   –   pupils and teachers must act on the identified problem

Realistic   –   targets must be possible within the home/school

Time-limited   –   everyone must be clear about the time-scale within which the targets are to be reached.

To what extent do your own action plans fulfil these objectives?

This page can be photocopied. © *Managing Special Educational Needs*, Gibson and Blandford, 2005

IEPs will need to be reviewed at least twice a year, but ideally each term or possibly more frequently for some pupils. At least one review in the year could coincide with a parents' evening, although schools should recognise that some parents will prefer a private meeting. Reviews need not be unduly formal, but parents' views on the child's progress should be sought and they should be consulted as part of the review process. Wherever possible, the pupil should also take part in the review process and be involved in setting the targets. If the pupil is not involved in the review, her/his ascertainable views should be considered in any discussion.

Reviews must happen. It is important that the review date is adhered to and that each participant is given the opportunity to report back, leading to an overall discussion of progress. The most common outcomes should be the identification of:

- what worked well and why

- the difficulties and how such difficulties can be overcome

- new areas of concern and new targets for action.

A successful education plan will leave all participants feeling that they are in control and are confident of achieving their goal for the pupil. Strategies employed to enable the pupil to progress should be recorded within an IEP. Further information on managing IEPs and group education plans can be found in the SEN Toolkit (DfES, 2001c).

ACTIVITY 6.5: INDIVIDUAL EDUCATION PLANS

Individual Education Plans should include information about:

- the short-term targets set for or by the pupil

- the teaching strategies to be used

- the provision to be put in place

- when the plan is to be reviewed

- success and/or exit criteria

- outcomes.

Evaluate your own practice in relation to the above.

This page can be photocopied. © *Managing Special Educational Needs*, Gibson and Blandford, 2005

The IEP should only record that which is additional to, or different from, the differentiated curriculum plan as part of provision for all pupils. The IEP should be crisply written and focus on three or four individual targets, chosen from those relating to the key areas of communication, literacy, mathematics, and behaviour and social skills that match the pupil's needs. The IEP should be discussed with the pupil and the parents.

Section Four: Case study

The following family-based case study illustrates how positive practices can enhance pupils' attitudes towards school.

Coping with Kids

This was a successful project focusing on parental skills and aimed to help children develop the motivation, self-control and responsibility necessary to become effective future members of society by providing support to their parents through a short series of workshops and discussion groups. The aims of the project (Robinson, 1997) were to:

- provide a network of workshops for parents focused on managing children's behaviour

- work at a multi-agency level to provide workshops and venues in a variety of community locations and to support the most vulnerable families to attend the sessions

- allow open access to all parents in the locality, irrespective of income, ethnic background, gender or disability

- provide leadership training on a regular basis to enable suitably qualified adults already working in the community to lead the workshops

- continue developing and adapting training materials to provide the best possible support for both parents and leaders.

Individual workshops were held to support and encourage positive, caring and happy family life in order to enable parents to cope effectively with challenging behaviour, within the principles laid out in the United Nations (1989) *Convention on the Rights of the Child*. Each session provided an opportunity for mutual discussion and support between parents.

Each course was evaluated by the participants and leaders at the end of the third session. In practice, over two hundred families benefited from 'Coping with Kids' courses during 1996–97, with 50 per cent of these being drawn from the lowest income sector. Evaluations by both participants and leaders were very positive and the quality of the workshops was further demonstrated by the low drop-out rate (seven per cent). There was a demand for more workshops and many course leaders now run them on a regular basis from their own centres. The impact on behaviour and school attendance was monitored; significant improvements were noted in all cases. This illustrates the positive impact of joint activities between parents and LEA services.

Executive summary

- The need for multi-agency consultation and communication in support of pupils with SEN is self-evident.

- The wealth of support available to pupils and teachers for support of pupils with SEN is a significant reflection of the need for schools to provide a safe and secure environment for all members of the school community.

- Meeting the SEN of individual children requires flexible working of statutory agencies. They need to communicate and agree policies and protocols which ensure that there is a seamless service.

- Services should adopt a flexible pupil-centred approach to service delivery to ensure that the changing needs and priorities of the child and her/his parents can be met at any given time.

- The SENCO should be aware of the LEA's policy for the provision of support services and how the school can access them.

- The educational psychology team is central to the planning of multi-agency support for pupils and families with behaviour problems.

■ Voluntary agencies and groups have an important role to play in meeting the needs of pupils with SEN.

■ Individual Education Plans (IEPs) provide teachers and support agencies with a joint framework for supporting a pupil with SEN. IEPs are a useful mechanism for evaluating the needs of pupils with learning or behavioural problems.

■ A successful education plan will leave all participants feeling that they are in control and are confident of achieving their goal for the pupil.

Further reading

Blamires, M. and Moore, J. (2004), *Support Services and Mainstream Schools*, London: David Fulton Publishers
Blandford, S. (1998), *Managing Discipline in Schools,* London: Routledge
Blandford, S. (2003), *School Discipline Manual*, London: Pearson Education
Lacey, P. (2001), *Support Partnerships: Collaboration in Action*, London: David Fulton Publishers

A Policy for Practice

7

CHAPTER 7: KEY QUESTIONS TO BE CONSIDERED
■ What should a democratic school management system aim to achieve through a policy for SEN?
■ How can a school be effective and inclusive?
■ How can inclusive values and policies encourage overall school improvement?
■ How does such a school ensure effective procedures for monitoring and evaluating policy impact?

Introduction

This chapter provides senior leaders, SENCOs and the SEN team with an introduction to creating, writing and implementing a SEN policy. Specifically, it considers how to draw on the expertise of those involved in working with pupils with SEN, which in practice involves the whole-school community and external agencies. The importance of planning and contextualising the policy will be discussed prior to the writing of the policy. This chapter will also provide the practitioner with insight into school development planning relating to inclusion.

Schools should move towards seeing themselves as learning organisations promoting a culture that celebrates difference and collegiality. Members of the school community will feel valued and positive about their work when they are involved in its development. To enhance the professional work of teachers, monitoring and evaluation of policies and development needs to be clear and useful. The question is how does the SEN policy enhance teaching and learning and does it lead to overall school improvement? Hence a review process must include all aspects of policy implementation and development. The chapter is presented in five sections:

- ■ Section One: Democratic school management

- ■ Section two: Effective and inclusive schools

- ■ Section Three: Creating and implementing a SEN policy

- ■ Section Four: Monitoring and evaluating policy

- ■ Section Five: Setting targets for pupils with SEN

The problems and challenges in developing and implementing an effective SEN policy are self-evident. This chapter will guide and support those responsible for the process.

School SEN policies are not stand-alone; they interact with a range of LEA policies including those relating to education welfare, emotional and behavioural difficulty support, social services and health. As indicated in Chapter 6, a SEN policy written without consultation with internal and external agencies will fail to benefit from the professional support that exists within the education service.

Section One: Democratic school management

To create an effective SEN policy team, schools need to address their current culture, style and attitudes towards leadership and management (see Chapter 5). Democratic and inclusive leadership is that which listens to and acts upon the voices of all groups in the community. The policy team needs to formulate awareness of established norms and culture before embarking on developing a policy that impacts on the school community.

KEY QUESTIONS
These questions attempt to view culture within your school.   ■ How are decisions made in our school?   ■ How do things happen in our school community?   ■ Who has power?   ■ Who has a voice?   ■ Do we work together or is management style divisive?   ■ Do we consider the whole-school community in our decision-making processes or do we confine this to consideration of the school solely as institution?

Once these questions have been asked the school leadership team will need to consider how to develop a school community policy for inclusion. Table 7.1 shows a template to promote and establish the school community as a learning community which has a foundation of common understandings and values enabling inclusive leadership and practices.

Table 7.1 A school community policy for inclusion

1. Head teacher to liaise with SENCO and heads of department, TAs, Parent–Teacher Association (PTA), pupils' school council or prefects and LEA in order to establish a school Inclusion Policy Team (IPT).

2. Representation from each element of school community ensures all voices are heard, thus whole-school community needs and perspectives considered.

3. Liaison to focus on the desire and need for the school community to formulate an inclusion policy using the revised CoP, current local and national government policy, incentives and academic research.

4. Team to ascertain strengths and weaknesses of school community in relation to the revised CoP, current local and national government policy, incentives and academic research.

5. Team to revise school mission statement in accordance with their assessment of school's strengths and weaknesses.

6. Mission statement to emphasis community's strengths in meeting the needs of all learners, CPD for teachers, noting where and how the school community can continue to develop.

7. Inclusion policy to stem from the ethos of school's mission statement denoting strengths and areas for growth.

8. Targets emerging from the policy are established, such as:
   - providing all practitioners with relevant CPD, i.e. that which is deemed necessary by both practitioner and IPT
   - ensuring all pupils at *School Action* and *School Action Plus* stages on the revised CoP are reviewed regularly, with reviews and amendments communicated to all teachers via heads of departments.

9. Time-scale for targets relating to policy are established.

10. Targets noted and information kept on file for annual evaluation meeting. Targets will be in relation to outcome such as:
    - teacher feedback after CPD provision
    - heads of departments' feedback regarding communication from SENCO on pupil's IEP reviews.

11. IPT to meet regularly, i.e. monthly meetings. These meetings are primarily for the purpose of monitoring the policy's implementation.

12. Evaluation of policy may be annual or biannual depending on school community's needs.

13. Evaluation meetings compile all feedback relating to targets established in the policy. In particular, that information indicating success and/or failure of policy initiatives is noted and an alternative or continuation of initiative established.

Inclusion is not to be viewed or understood as an end point or product emergent when a teacher or school uses a particular formula in teaching or management. It is not a restricted theory; inclusion results in processes which take the school community on a journey, where decisions are made and approaches adopted on the basis of social justice as understood and practised by its members. Such processes will result in the establishment of a learning community and a democratic school.

Section Two: Effective and inclusive schools

SEN policies are context bound. The current context for educational practitioners is that of effective and inclusive schools. School effectiveness literature has grown since the early 1980s (Lunt and Norwich, 1999; Frederickson and Cline, 2002). It stems from the school of thought which places the school as the primary agent, as opposed to the family and/or local community, in the pupil's development and success (Reynolds, 1995). Effective schools can also be inclusive schools, suggesting that effective and improving schools will have a positive impact upon the development of pupils with SEN (Stoll 1991; Ramasut and Reynolds, 1993). Reynolds maintains that school effectiveness and inclusive practice can be observed together in mainstream schools. Indeed, Reynolds suggests that for schools to be effective, they need to adopt a social view towards pupils with SEN which will inevitably embrace change that secures their development towards an inclusive model.

Lunt and Norwich (1999) advise that in order to determine what makes an effective and inclusive school, leaders must challenge the received model of school effectiveness. The received model is one that focuses solely on impact of the immediate school environment upon each pupil's learning and development. The received model also identities effective schools in terms of optimising outcomes for the majority, which is reflected by the perceived importance of government league tables, which merely illustrate a quantifiable approach to outcome and pupil achievement. It is self-evident that, given that pupils with SEN form a minority of the mainstream school population, defining and planning for school development based on the received model of school effectiveness will not necessarily lead to inclusive schools (Rea and Weiner, 1998; Blandford and Gibson, 2000).

The contextual model of school effectiveness provides an alternative model to the received model. The contextual model acknowledges the impact of external forces on school effectiveness, thus embracing the school community through its social and environmental setting. The contextual model acknowledges the importance of factors outside the school and their impact upon teaching and learning.

A third model, the catholic model of school effectiveness, provides a further alternative to the quantitative assessment basis of the received model. Grace (1998, p. 120) comments:

An argument is made that school effectiveness literature and research needs to be more catholic in the sense of being more comprehensive, universal and inclusive in the range of school outcomes, which are taken seriously.

In the context of developing an effective and inclusive school, Grace suggests that school mission statements are of crucial importance. Mission statements set out what a school's intended outcomes are for its pupils, their development and overall attainments – academic, social and personal. Such goals are not all quantifiable but some may demand a more qualitative case history approach in the assessment and analysis of their impact on practice. As Grace (1998, p. 121) states:

> *This could be the beginning ... of a more democratic, more flexible, more sensitive and more humane practice of school effectiveness research ... achieved by extending the important concept of 'value-added' research to include the equally important concept of 'value-added' inquiry.*

Case study: Birley Spa Primary School

An example of the catholic model in practice leading to enhanced school effectiveness and inclusion is Birley Spa Primary School in Sheffield. School development plans and a policy of inclusion were devised, implemented, monitored and evaluated by a school steering committee, which included senior and middle leadership teams, teachers, teaching assistants, parents, pupils, governors, local schools and LEA (Sharron, 2003). Thus the responsibility for establishing and maintaining an effective and inclusive school culture was shared by the community, as Sharron states (2003, p. 27):

> *Creating inclusive management structures whereby support staff, lunchtime supervisors, parents and pupils all understand the issues and are involved in working out policies for the school, has constructed a consensus around supporting very difficult children ... Distributed leadership is the current catchphrase for what Birley Spa is undertaking.*

Practitioners at this school found that they were able to take innovative approaches in supporting all pupils; this included problem-based learning and the development of approaches to preferred learning styles.

As the authors have indicated, it is imperative to establish and provide for the learning needs of AUP practitioners within the context of school development. An interesting outcome of developments at Birley Spa was that over 50 per cent of staff were registered on a Masters in Education programme and half the TAs on NVQ courses. A clear outcome was that the school had improved in Standard Assessment Test (SAT) results and was described by OfSTED inspectors as *outstanding*.

Section Three: Creating and implementing a SEN policy

Every school should have a school improvement plan that provides a framework for strategic planning which identifies long- and short-term objectives; a SEN policy will be linked to this overall plan. The plan should relate clearly to the school vision and be central to school management by involving all teachers in the process of identifying its aims and objectives. The plan should also encompass other school initiatives. All policies need to reflect school, LEA and government policies. The main purpose of any plan should be to improve the quality of teaching and learning for all pupils.

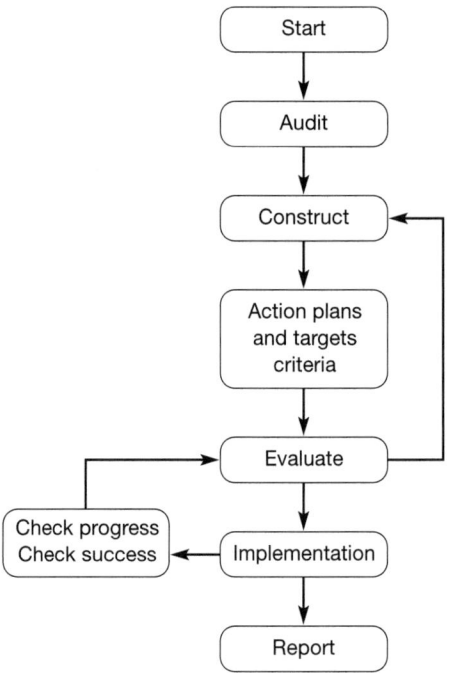

Figure 7.1 The planning process (Blandford, 1997)

Strategic planning occurs annually through the school improvement plan; this is a suitable time to review whether the school is an inclusive school and has suitable policies for pupils with SEN. Figure 7.1 illustrates the planning process. The creation of a SEN policy is central to the management of all learners in schools. In most cases, if a class or pupil is deemed to be of little value to the school community, the response of the class or individual will be to behave in an unacceptable manner and so SEN is linked to developing a learning environment for a community of learners. A fundamental element of learning and teaching is the self-esteem of pupil, teacher and senior leadership team. Without self-esteem, pupils and teachers will not function in the school community. There is a need for every school to have a SEN policy that focuses on personal development and growth. As explained in the previous section, a SEN policy should reflect the ethos of the school and contribute to the fulfilment of its mission.

In practice, a SEN policy should reflect the values and beliefs of the school community. It should also relate to the social development of pupils as appropriate to their age and personal needs. Examples of school values as practised by the school community have been listed by OfSTED (1995) and include:

- telling the truth and keeping promises

- respecting the rights and property of others

- acting considerately towards others

- helping those less fortunate and weaker than ourselves

- taking personal responsibility for one's actions.

This example demonstrates the importance of an inclusive community and the need for schools to develop their own ethos and sense of community. Therefore each school will need to have a view on what they wish to encourage. Schools will need to encourage the development of desirable attitudes and personal qualities which can relate to the knowledge and understanding, skills and abilities of the members of their community.

The development of personal values is an outcome of an effective SEN policy that relates to the social function of each school. Schools complement and extend the functions of the home and wider community by helping to prepare all pupils to live in society. Pupils need to learn the obligations that go with membership of a group and a community. Pupils also need to become aware of their own identity as individuals and of the importance of taking account of the feelings and wishes of others.

In practice, teachers provide a range of opportunities for pupils to learn and develop social skills and attitudes. The process of social development is continued throughout primary and secondary education, in school rules and codes of practice, in school councils and clubs and in the encouragement of pupils' responsibility for themselves and others.

Teachers will benefit greatly from a clear and agreed SEN policy that has expectations of them as practitioners. Effective teachers operating under clearly understood guidelines will feel confident in giving clear instructions and presentations, having precise work requirements of pupils, handling different situations quickly and calmly, and ensuring that work is appropriate to pupils' abilities.

The precise content of a SEN policy must be determined by the school community. Following the recommendations from the DfES (2001a), whole-school SEN policies should be simple, straightforward and based on a clear set of principles and values.

What makes a good SEN policy?

There is a huge difference for the teacher between simply having a SEN policy on paper, and having one that actually works well in practice. Here are some factors that go towards making a policy work for the classroom teacher, whereby the policy is:

- not just a paper exercise, but is used effectively on a daily basis and across the whole school

- created in consultation with teachers and pupils

- reviewed and updated to ensure that any parts which do not work are altered

- clear to pupils, parents and staff

- a clear and effective part of the whole-school ethos

- one that puts the emphasis on positive aspects

- one that lets teachers know what to do, and who to turn to, if additional help is needed

- one that encourages consistency, but also allows for individual approaches to SEN.

In practice, a SEN policy should be a comprehensive and assertive statement intended to guide the school community (Johnson et al., 1994). The policy should be the outcome of a democratic decision-making process involving all members of the school community; participation is the key to an effective policy. Senior managers should begin the process of developing a policy by:

- identifying the stages of development

- identifying key personnel; SENCO and a SEN team responsible for writing the policy

- deciding on a time-scale for short-, medium- and long-term objectives

- identifying achievable outcomes related to the school vision and development plan

- identifying professional development support and INSET needs for the whole staff.

Decision-making

The process of developing and implementing a SEN policy will involve collaborative decision-making. Participation in decision-making is critical to the success of any policy and time must be allocated. Participation in decision-making is a new phenomenon in schools; devolution of power through the LMS and the National Curriculum has led to a greater level of participation. In practice, decisions may be above the mandate of individual teachers or working groups; however, participation will increase the likelihood of successful implementation of a SEN policy.

ACTIVITY 7.1: GUIDANCE ON POLICY DEVELOPMENT	
Do you and your team have the knowledge and understanding to develop school policies that will be inclusive and raise achievement?	
AIM – Raising achievement: developing a SEN policy Objectives:	
▨ The SEN policy will be published and become the basis of practice for all staff.	Y/N
▨ Training in SEN strategies will be made available to all staff and disseminated.	Y/N
▨ Display areas will be created throughout the school and pupils' work and records of activities put on exhibition to make corridors reflect the life and ethos of the school.	Y/N
▨ A professional counselling service will be made available to pupils.	Y/N
AIM – Raising achievement of pupils with SEN: improving management Objectives:	
▨ A new and wider forum for discussion of the curriculum and other SEN issues will have been established.	Y/N
▨ Members of the SEN team will have been linked to all subjects to provide a clear line of communication, monitor standards and offer support.	Y/N
▨ A revised pattern of meetings will be introduced, increasing the number of task groups and increasing the number of whole-staff, subject and year team meetings to discuss SEN developments.	Y/N
▨ Guidance from the revised CoP (DfES, 2001a) will be used as a benchmark for the development of in-service training, planning and communication.	Y/N

© *Managing Special Educational Needs*, Gibson and Blandford, 2005

Section Four: How to monitor, review and evaluate a SEN policy

Inclusion is not something that can be made to happen from outside a school or even by the commitment of a few dedicated individuals. It requires ownership by the head teacher and senior leadership team, governors and all staff. It also requires willingness on the part of schools to look at their own practice and to identify areas where they could do better. Inclusion must be an integral part of whole-school self-evaluation and improvement. Many local authorities have agreed self-evaluation frameworks with their schools and the following range of tools can be used by schools to assess how well they are serving different groups of pupils, including those with SEN:

- OfSTED's inspection handbook.

- *Evaluating Educational Inclusion* (OfSTED, 2000).

- Primary National Strategy – materials to link with existing self-evaluation frameworks for subject leaders and key stage co-ordinators.

- *Index for Inclusion* – designed to help schools to assess how inclusive they are and to support their development; explains the concepts behind inclusion and provides a detailed framework for self-review and materials to support it (CSIE, 2004).

- Quality in Schools materials (booklet and CD-ROM) – they have been developed by LloydsTSB and contain tools that a school can use for self-assessment and improvement planning, including self-review in relation to provision for pupils with SEN and inclusion.

The method by which a school meets the needs of all pupils has a direct bearing on the nature of the additional and different support required by pupils with SEN and on the point at which additional support is given. The key to meeting the needs of all pupils lies in the teacher's knowledge of each child's skills and abilities and the teacher's ability to match this knowledge to finding ways of providing appropriate participation and engagement with the curriculum for every child.

It is for individual schools to decide the procedures they should adopt for meeting the needs of all pupils, for observing and assessing their progress, and for deciding the nature of the special educational provision. It is essential that these procedures are carefully managed and monitored, and that there are effective internal communication and liaison arrangements between staff. Systems for establishing communication, such as the role of the IPT, will be addressed.

A school's system for observing and assessing the progress of individual pupils should provide information on where a child is not progressing satisfactorily even though learning styles and presentation of information have been differentiated. These observations should be enhanced by knowledge of an individual child's strengths and weaknesses. Using this evidence, class teachers may see that current strategies are not resulting in the child learning as effectively as possible. Under these circumstances, they will need to consult the SENCO to consider what else might be done. The starting point will always be a review of the current strategies and the way in which these might be developed. The review may lead to the conclusion that the pupil requires help over and above that which is normally available within the particular class or subject. Adequate progress can be defined in a number of ways. It might be progress that:

- closes the attainment gap between the child and her/his peers

- prevents the attainment gap growing wider

- matches or betters the child's previous rate of progress

- ensures access to the full curriculum

◼ demonstrates an improvement in self-help, social or personal skills

◼ demonstrates improvements in the child's behaviour.

Monitoring and evaluation is critical to the successful implementation of a policy for inclusion. This will involve senior and middle leadership teams, teachers, TAs, parents, pupils governors and LEA. If a policy is not monitored and evaluated, it will not be possible to determine whether objectives have been achieved. The process of monitoring will also enable members of the school community to move further towards agreed objectives. Once a collegial approach to policy development, monitoring and evaluation has been adopted, the school community can move forward with confidence.

Monitoring must be based on practice and outcomes, and related to agreed criteria/set targets. Furthermore it should provide a framework in which teachers can reflect on their own practice and professional needs.

In contrast to monitoring, evaluation entails reviewing the status of the policy aims. Through the evaluation process, the school community will be able to determine the need to change. As Hall and Oldroyd (1990) advise, evaluation is a collaborative exercise involving:

◼ asking questions

◼ gathering information

◼ forming conclusions

in order to:

◼ make recommendations

◼ deduce how successful implementations are.

When evaluating their inclusion policy, the school community must reconsider its purpose, content, procedures, context and outcomes. If there is a recognised need to change the purpose of the policy, the policy must be rewritten. The context in which the school may also be adapting to changing circumstances, for example new staff, new buildings or increased numbers, also needs to be considered. The inclusion policy must reflect such changes.

Section Five: Setting targets for pupils with SEN

Having written a policy for SEN, the SEN team should focus on policies for setting targets for pupils with SEN. Since the mid-1970s, successive governments have refined the statutory framework for pupils with SEN. This strategy aims to personalise learning for all pupils and make education more innovative and responsive to their diverse needs, so reducing a reliance on SEN structures and processes that are located outside school policies and thereby raising the achievement of the pupils – nearly one in six – who are considered to have SEN.

The revised CoP sets out the government's vision for the education of pupils with SEN. It provides clear national leadership supported by an ambitious programme of sustained action and review, nationally and locally, over a number of years, in four key areas:

- **Early intervention** – to ensure that pupils who have difficulties learning receive the help they need as soon as possible and that parents of pupils with SEN have access to suitable childcare

- **Removing barriers to learning** – by embedding inclusive practice in every school and early years setting

- **Raising expectations and achievement** – by developing teachers' skills and strategies for meeting the needs of pupils with SEN and sharpening our focus on the progress made by pupils with SEN

- **Delivering improvements in partnership** – taking a hands-on approach to improvement so that parents can be confident that their child will get the education he/she needs.

Within the context of such policies the government have provided guidance on setting targets for pupils with SEN. Such guidelines need to be considered within the context of writing a SEN policy.

Many schools see the importance of setting individual targets and recording progress in terms of personal and social development, but not many do so systematically. Most schools use target-setting to inform performance management, though they do not always link teachers' performance to evidence of improved pupil performance. The role of governors in overseeing target-setting, including those pupils with SEN, is currently underdeveloped and should be considered by the head teacher and chair of governors.

Although moderation of teacher assessment for the majority of pupils is satisfactory across most schools, it is underdeveloped in relation to the assessment of pupils with SEN. Special schools have increasing expertise in teacher assessment using P levels, and in some areas this is being shared effectively with mainstream schools and LEA officers.

Target-setting has the greatest impact when it focuses on precise curriculum objectives for individuals and when it forms part of a whole-school improvement process. In a survey, eight out of ten maintained special schools set and published statutory performance targets (OFSTED, 2004). Almost all special schools use performance levels to assess individual pupils and set their targets, although they face difficulties in setting targets realistically for attainment five terms ahead in order to meet statutory requirements. Schools for pupils with Profound and Multiple Learning Difficulties (PMLD) experience particular difficulties in this respect. Special schools need more support from LEAs if they are to set up effective information systems to track pupils' progress and analyse data over time.

Mainstream schools are not required to set performance targets for pupils who are unlikely to achieve national expectations. Many are able to do so as they have developed expertise in tracking pupils' progress and analysing school performance data, but they do not always do this for pupils with SEN. However, the Audit Commission's report

Special Educational Needs: a mainstream issue (Audit Commission, 2002) highlighted a number of continuing challenges:

- too many pupils wait for too long to have their needs met

- pupils who should be able to be taught in mainstream settings are sometimes turned away and many staff feel ill-equipped to meet the wide range of pupil needs in today's classrooms

- many special schools feel uncertain of their future role

- families face unacceptable variations in the level of support available from their school, local authority or local health services.

Much of the above is rooted in the need to improve and enhance staff development (see Chapter 8).

Executive summary

- School effectiveness and inclusive practice can occur together once schools adopt an inclusive view in relation to the education of pupils with SEN.

- The contextual and catholic models of school effectiveness recognise the impact of external forces on school effectiveness.

- A school community that learns together, promoting the importance of knowledge, growth and the development of new and/or enhanced skills, will reflect the values and ethos of an effective and inclusive community.

- Monitoring and evaluation of SEN policies is critical to successful implementation and policy impact.

- The SEN policy team will be responsible for devising, implementing, monitoring, and evaluating policies for SEN.

- Inclusive leadership is that which listens to and acts upon the voices of all groups in the community.

- Inclusion results in processes, which take the school community on a journey, a journey where decisions are made and approaches adopted on the basis of inclusion.

- The school community that grows and manages together will reflect the values and ethos of inclusion, an ongoing developmental process effecting and affected by contextual issues within and beyond the school.

- Policy development, implementation, monitoring and evaluation are managed processes.

Further reading

Bradbury, I., O'Neill, J. and West-Burnham, J. (2001), *Performance Management in Schools*, London: Pearson Education

Bush, T. and Bell, L.A. (eds) (2002), *The Principles and Practice of Educational Management*, London: Paul Chapman Publishing

West-Burnham, J. (1997) *Managing Quality in Schools*, London: Pearson Education

Professional Development in an Inclusive and Effective School

CHAPTER 8: KEY QUESTIONS TO BE CONSIDERED
■ How can inclusive values and policies be adopted by staff?
■ How do AUP practitioners establish what their CPD needs are?
■ How do inclusive school communities undertake, monitor and evaluate INSET?

Introduction

Teachers are responsible for the development of pupil knowledge, citizenship and values, but if they do not have the opportunity to develop themselves, they will not succeed in the classroom. The professional development of teachers and managers is often determined by school leaders. From initial teacher training to retirement, teachers often lack the support and guidance afforded other professionals. Yet teachers are responsible for embedding notions of life-long learning in pupils. What is clear from the research underpinning this book is the need for teachers to be developed as holistic practitioners beyond the subject or key stage. Schools that develop staff will grow as learning organisations.

The common problems and questions that mainstream practitioners, teachers and managers have regarding SEN issues often arise because of a lack of staff development. Links between policy and professional development are critical to the implementation of effective practice.

This chapter focuses on the professional development needs of practitioners that moves beyond Initial Teacher Education (ITE), recognising educational policies and relationships with other agencies. Schools are learning organisations that celebrate difference and collegiality. To enhance the professional work of teachers, an understanding of professional development is essential. With effective professional development, members of the school community will feel valued and positive about their work when they are involved in its development. The chapter is presented in six sections:

- Section One: Developing an AUP practitioner
- Section Two: Mentoring
- Section Three: Teaching Assistants
- Section Four: Planning whole-school professional development
- Section Five: INSET
- Section Six: Evaluating INSET.

Section One: Developing an AUP practitioner

The method by which a school meets the needs of all children has a direct bearing on the nature of the additional and different support required by pupils with SEN. The key to meeting the needs of all children lies in the teacher's knowledge of each child's skills and abilities and her/his ability to relate this knowledge to appropriate ways of engaging with learning and teaching.

Self-development is systematic; teachers are also learners who never stop learning and developing. The art of self-evaluation is to be continually learning. Senge (1990, p. 142) makes it clear:

> *People with a high level of personal mastery live in a continual learning mode. They never 'arrive'. People with a high level of personal mastery are acutely aware of their ignorance, their incompetence, their growth areas. And they are deeply self-confident.*

The culture of the teaching profession is changing, reflecting the changing society in which we live, with its proliferation of cultures, beliefs and values. Effective teaching and learning in schools is based on shared beliefs and values. The school community works towards a common goal, reaching for and achieving targets. In practice, teachers need to relate their actions to their beliefs and values. If the two do not equate, teachers should consider their position in the school in relation to pupils' needs. Schools should be places in which success is celebrated, the blame culture prevalent in the 1980s replaced by the caring culture of the 1990s and beyond. How does this happen? Do teachers willingly participate in the change process, or are they passive in their response to the dominant ideology of the day? While these are matters of sociological debate, self-evaluation and effective self-development should influence practice in a positive way. A starting-point for this process could inform practitioners about their individual aspirations in terms of their career.

KEY QUESTIONS

- What do I value?

- What is my present situation?

- Where would I like my career to lead?

- How might I get there?

- What help is available?

- Do I have ability to self-manage?

- Do I have clear personal values and objectives?

- Do I have an emphasis on continuing personal growth?

- Do I have effective problem-solving skills?

- Do I have the capacity to be creative and innovative?

A fundamental issue will be individuals' ability to recognise where they are in relation to where they would like to be. As Senge indicated, the most successful among us will never reach their destiny. Self-evaluation of professional competence is more than an assessment of traditional conformity or technical accountability. It is assessed in terms of moral and prudent answerability for practical judgements actually made within the context of existing educational institutions (Carr and Kemmis, 1986, p. 31).

A means of developing the skills required for self-evaluation is to consider the range of knowledge that exists regarding educational practice:

- common-sense knowledge about practice that is simply assumption or opinion, for example the view that students need discipline

- folk-wisdom of teachers, like the view that pupils get restless on windy days

- skill knowledge used by teachers: how to line pupils up, or how to prevent pupils speaking while instructions about a task are being given

- contextual knowledge: the background knowledge about this class, this community or pupil, against which aspirations are measured

- professional knowledge about teaching strategies and curriculum

- educational theory: ideas about the development of individuals, or about the role of education in society

- social and moral theories and general philosophical outlooks: about how people can and should interact, the uses of knowledge in society, or about truth and justice.

Theory and knowledge can transform a teacher's beliefs and values. In the process of self-reflection, interaction with educational theory may not dictate practice, but it may transform the outlook of the practitioner. Providing individuals with new concepts is a means not merely to offer them a new way of thinking, but also to offer them the possibility of becoming more self-aware of their thoughts and actions. The full task of self-reflection and evaluation requires teachers to collaborate in decision-making that will transform their situation. The process of self-evaluation encompasses the interaction of the teacher with the school. Teachers should consider whether they are in the right school for them. In brief, there are positive outcomes of collaborative CPD which include:

- self-confidence

- knowledge and understanding of pupils' learning

- capacity to draw on a wide range of teaching and learning strategies to match pupils' needs

- willingness and ability to make changes in practice

- self-efficacy – their belief in their ability to make a difference.

Self-development involves learning and understanding where you are within your job and career. Practitioners should, as stated, have a clear view of what their job is about: the relationship between teaching, leadership and management, self-development planning (SDP) and so on. Practitioners should also have an understanding of their position in relation to those they manage. For a practitioner, self-development can be difficult. Practitioners face many demands, including:

- government demands: deliver the curriculum, register pupils, parents' evenings

- senior management demands: implementation – action of school policy

- colleagues' demands: requests for assistance, information or help from others at a similar level or within your team

- pupils' demands: to inform and liaise

- parents' and governors' demands

- externally imposed demands: social services, police, agencies which work for and with young people

- system-imposed demands: LMS, LEA, budgets, meetings, and social functions, which cannot be ignored.

In addition, there will be other demands such as family, friends, hobbies and social commitments. It is important to understand that teachers and support staff need a balance between their professional and personal lives.

ACTIVITY 8.1: SELF-DEVELOPMENT

As a starting-point, practitioners could begin by considering the factors influencing self-development:

- use of environment
- environment for learning
- resource development and management
- classroom control
- teaching performance
- rapport with pupils

- lesson organisation
- promotion of learning
- flexibility
- subject competence
- pastoral competence
- professional approach.

This page can be photocopied. © *Managing Special Educational Needs*, Gibson and Blandford, 2005

Section Two: Mentoring

In establishing a starting-point for staff development, an AUP practitioner might be assigned a mentor who will act as an enabler, helping the practitioner to locate strengths and areas needing development. Mentors are likely to have a number of roles within the school and they need to decide who to mentor in the context of their other tasks and responsibilities. It is recommended that in the context of supporting CPD in the area of managing SEN, practitioners be assigned a mentor representative from the school Inclusion Policy Team (see Chapter 7). Mentoring is a positive mechanism for developing skills for both the mentor and mentee. As a process, mentoring should move through the stages outlined in Figure 8.1.

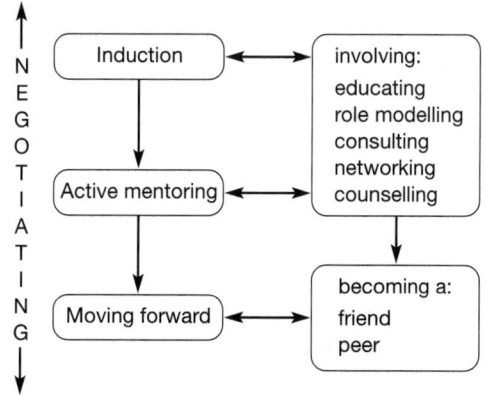

Figure 8.1 A Model of Mentoring (Blandford, 2004)

Mentoring is a term which is used in several different contexts in education (Ormston and Shaw, 1993). It generally means the positive support offered by staff with some experience to staff with less experience of the school. This experience can extend over a wide range of activities, or be specific to one activity. Activity 8.2 suggests activities for mentor and mentee, which will enable the mentee to ascertain what her/his CPD needs are and to decide how best to meet them.

ACTIVITY 8.2: DECIDING AND ACTING ON THE PROFESSIONAL DEVELOPMENT NEEDS OF THE AUP PRACTITIONER

Areas to be addressed	Action to be taken
Observing other practitioners: Have you had the opportunity to observe other colleagues? Have you had the opportunity to shadow a colleague and/or observe a visiting expert?	
Expanding on professional experience: Have you been involved in providing any INSET? What roles and responsibilities or contributions do you feel you are currently making to the SEN team? How would you like to contribute (if at all) to this work? Are you involved in the school community in the form of governor and/or union representative? Have you been involved in any team teaching with colleagues and/or TAs? Have you been involved in mentoring NQTs?	
Working with pupils: Have you been enabled to expand on and develop your teaching skills? Have you had responsibility for off-site work with pupils? Have you been involved as mentor to or facilitator of pupils' school council?	
Working with your school community: Do you liaise with pupils' parents/guardians? Have you ever been involved in a community initiative involving colleagues, pupils, youth workers, TA, LEA, and/or parents?	

Areas to be addressed	Action to be taken
If yes, what did this initiative entail and, from the perspective of inclusion, do you consider it to be a success? How are you and/or could you be involved in the school community that extends beyond the school as 'institution'?	
Evaluating your practice(s): Have you had observation of your teaching? Have you accessed feedback on teaching and/or classroom environment from your pupils? How do you make use of ICT either in lesson planning or directly in the classroom? How do you ensure marking is reviewed or moderated?	

This page can be photocopied. © *Managing Special Educational Needs*, Gibson and Blandford, 2005

Mentors are likely to have a number of roles within the school and they need to decide whom to mentor in the context of their other tasks and responsibilities. Mentoring is time consuming. Mentees should select their mentor based on professional needs, present and/or future. It is important to understand that mentoring is a continuous staff development activity which, once the system is established, takes place during normal school life. Mentors need to know and understand the essential elements of a mentoring relationship, as outlined in Table 8.1.

Table 8.1 The essential elements of mentoring

- a recognised procedure, formal or informal
- a clear understanding of the procedure and the roles of mentor and mentee
- trust and a rapport between both parties
- the credibility and genuineness of the mentor as perceived by the mentee
- confidentiality and discretion
- a relationship based on the mentee's perception of her/his own needs
- a suitable range of skills used by the mentor: counselling, listening, sensitive questioning, analysis and handing back responsibilities
- an appropriate attitude by both parties, for example the ability of the mentor to challenge the mentee, and the self-motivation of the mentee to take action when necessary
- In addition, teachers should be aware of equal opportunity issues that need to be addressed in the selection and training of mentors.

Activity 8.3 sets out how to create an effective mentoring scheme to support teaching staff in their development as AUP practitioners. It is suggested this activity be undertaken by the school SEN team in consultation with senior management.

ACTIVITY 8.3: CREATING A MENTOR SCHEME

- Make all staff and governors aware of the scheme. This limits:
  - animosity from teachers who are not on the mentor programme
  - antagonism of middle management if teachers in their department/teams sometimes have mentors elsewhere in the school
  - anxiety of governors who may see it as a system for 'favourites'.

- Nominate a senior (trained) member of staff to manage the scheme and to train members in skills such as coaching, guidance and counselling.

- Select teachers and mentors. Both should be volunteers, but some selection may be necessary. Teachers should be assertive, positive, willing to work hard and to learn. Mentors should be professionally expert, empathetic and have good interpersonal skills. They coach, encourage self-assessment, teach skills, encourage project work and innovation, argue and discuss.

- Pair up mentors with suitable teachers to maximise benefit. Draw the department head or manager into the process.

- Assess the success of the scheme, weighing the development of the teachers against the problems experienced. Ensure that mentors gain in credit, experience and in possible career prospects.

This page can be photocopied. © *Managing Special Educational Needs*, Gibson and Blandford, 2005

Section Three: Teaching Assistants (TAs)

The following extracts from SENCO Update, May 2004, describes the impact of the remodelled workforce on practice. TAs are now part of the central core of paraprofessionals who support practice in schools.

> Currently over 225,000 support staff work in English schools, providing a wide range of support to 430,000 teachers. Recently the Teacher Training Agency has launched two major initiatives to enhance the skills of these important members of the education workforce, and in so doing, is expanding its remit significantly.

Training is needed to support TAs. This is being provided through the Higher Level Teaching Assistants scheme which:

> ... *commenced in May 2004 when the first 7,000 candidates started training, to be followed by 7,000 in 2005–06 and another 7,000 in 2006–07. Participants*

in the training scheme will be trained to meet, and assessed against, national professional standards. Two training pathways will be available:

■ *An assessment-only pathway designed to allow teaching assistants who are already at, or near, the standards to achieve HLTA quickly*

■ *A full-training pathway running for 50 days designed to enable participants to meet the standards.*

Further training will be provided which extends beyond TAs and

... is focused on a wider conceptualisation of support work. In the coming year this will involve:

● *Clarifying the scope of the workforce encompassed by the new remit*

● *Agreeing with the other organisations a training and development framework for support staff, within the wider context of a children's agenda*

● *Establishing processes and machinery for decision-making and implementation*

● *Gathering data about staffing numbers, qualifications, training issues, standards and quality.*

From a special educational needs perspective, it would be useful if these activities considered how all support staff can assist the work of the SENCO.

Section Four: Planning whole-school professional development

The training of staff is critical to the development of a school's approach to inclusion and teaching pupils with SEN. INSET for teachers was considered by the government to be a suitable mechanism to implement development and, more specifically, change. Since the Education Reform Act (DES, 1988), five days per academic year have been allocated to staff development in all schools. The identification of need is the starting-point for any INSET; this begins with the analysis of training needs. When evaluating professional development needs (see Figure 8.1), practitioners should consider its purpose, context and pupil outcomes. If there is a recognised need to focus on one aspect of professional development, then action needs to be taken. The following criteria define an effective INSET (GTC, 1993):

■ recognition on the part of teachers of their training needs in relation to the objectives of the school and the LEA

■ support of the head teacher and other staff

■ a coherent school and LEA policy

■ precise targeting of provision

■ choice of appropriate form of INSET, whether school-based or externally based

■ fulfilment of appraisal targets

- choice of appropriate length of course and mode of attendance

- practical focus

- appropriate expertise on the part of the HEIs offering INSET

- the appropriate follow-up in schools.

An AUP practitioner will be a life-long learner, who will have an ongoing need to further develop academic, social and practical skills. Such practitioner professional development will be part of an overall plan or strategy within the school. INSET will provide the link between professional development and school development.

Professional development and INSET is specified as an important mechanism for achieving effective implementation of *Removing Barriers to Achievement* (DfES, 2004d). The plan for improving INSET and professional development opportunities requires action at three levels (Tod, 2004):

1. *Core Skills for all teachers in all schools to be addressed with the new QTS Standards and the Induction Standards for Qualified Teachers. Given the increase in QTS routes, it is likely that SENCOs will be required to support and mentor trainees as they now do for NQTs. It is anticipated that trainees will also be encouraged to observe good practice in special school settings.*

2. *Advanced skills for some teachers in all schools. LEAs will be encouraged to create a cadre of staff with particular expertise in SEN. They will be able to act as change champions in mainstream schools, special schools and pupil referral units across LEAs.*

3. *Specialist skills in some local schools. These are designed to support effective practice for pupils with particular needs in specialist or mainstream sectors. Examples given are for those pupils who pose particular challenges for inclusion into mainstream settings, e.g. severe learning difficulties and behavioural, emotional and social difficulties.*

ACTIVITY 8.4: PLANNING CPD IN YOUR SCHOOL COMMUNITY

Read through the list below and comment on how your school community currently carries out these practices. Effective CPD will be dependent on the management of:

- information – available for all staff concerning CPD programmes, INSET and Standards Funding for Education Support and Training

- planning – collaboration between multi-agencies in consultation with their teams

- evaluation – of all courses, teachers' needs in relation to pupils' needs and the school

- resources – utilisation of experts from LEA agencies, school, HEIs and other consultancies

- networking – the need for management and teachers to consult with teams and INSET providers.

The management of special educational needs would appear to relate directly to a range of expertise requiring quality training focusing on SEN-related issues for all staff. Activity 8.4 is to be carried out by senior management and the SEN team as a first stage in establishing effective professional development in their school community.

Activity 8.5 will provide individuals and teams with a deeper analysis of professional development needs and practice.

ACTIVITY 8.5: SEN PROFESSIONAL DEVELOPMENT PLAN

In this exercise, leaders and practitioners are to decide and plan on how to generate:

- a Total Quality environment that embraces inclusion
- a timeline to identify professional and organisational learning and development relating to TQM
- identification of available support for teachers within and beyond the school
- follow-up procedures, which consider the impact of new TQM practices through the discussion of evaluation evidence.

Timeline	Support agencies	Follow-up
Term 1 1. 2. 3. 4. 5.		1. 2. 3. 4. 5.
Term 2 1. 2. 3. 4. 5.		1. 2. 3. 4. 5.
Term 3 1. 2. 3. 4. 5.		1. 2. 3. 4. 5.

This page can be photocopied. © *Managing Special Educational Needs*, Gibson and Blandford, 2005

Section Five: INSET

When planning, implementing and reviewing INSET programmes, the focus should be on the relevance of the programme to enhancing practitioners' self-confidence in their ability to teach and manage the learning needs of all their pupils. Critically, INSET evaluations should reflect, inform and review policy; the process should involve:

■ an evaluation brief that will inform policy

■ a statement of aims

■ a list of performance indicators relating to targets that are SMART (Specific, Measurable, Attainable, Relevant and Time-limited).

■ detailed questions related to the above

■ information arising from the evaluation process that is related to practice

■ outcomes that are accessible to all staff

■ conclusions that will inform policy.

Senior leaders have a responsibility to see that individuals develop new skills. Staff development should not necessarily mean an additional activity; often development activities will happen as a matter of course. Staff development includes personal, team and school development. Staff development has a wider importance in:

■ promoting shared values

■ implementing change

■ promoting equal opportunities.

A team representing the views of all staff should plan INSET programmes. Once planned, the programme should be circulated and views sought from colleagues on appropriate approaches to each element. The final details should reflect staff needs and concerns. These should relate directly to pupil needs. INSET is only part of the process of developing, implementing and reviewing change. It is not a panacea for all ills but should be placed in the context of practice. If change is needed, it should be considered within the priorities of the school development plan.

A gap analysis between what is happening in school and what is intended to happen may show that there are divisions between:

■ actual and target performance indicators

■ the evidence of the school review and the school development plan

- school actual and planned results

- knowledge and skill possessed by staff and the knowledge and skill shown by job analysis

- actual appraised performance of individuals and the target performance.

Planning for INSET will require several months of review and consultation. Staff should not be expected to accommodate suggestions immediately. As professionals, teachers should view the place in which they work as a place of learning. Within the framework of CPD, self-development and staff development are prerequisites for effective management and effective schools. Equally, a precondition and an outcome of effective INSET is a culture that encourages reflection and development. Professional competencies of the successful AUP practitioner are identifiable as:

- Knowledge and understanding:

    - Knowledge of children and their learning

    - Subject knowledge

    - Knowledge of the curriculum

    - Knowledge of the teacher's role.

- Skills:

    - Subject application

    - Classroom methodology

    - Class management

    - Assessment and recording.

Essentially, an AUP practitioner should maintain a hunger for learning – learning that underpins practice ready to launch all pupils as life-long learners.

Section Six: Evaluating INSET

Evaluation of INSET plans acts as an overall check on whether objectives are achieved. Evaluation should be a collaborative process. The desire to achieve success is motivating; evaluation should focus on success in addition to identifying improvement areas. Evaluation is a component of development planning and prerequisite for preparing any subsequent plan. Table 8.2 sets out the purposes of evaluating INSET plans.

Table 8.2 The purpose of evaluating INSET plans

> ▪ To examine the success of the implementation of the plan.
>
> ▪ To assess the extent to which the aims have been furthered.
>
> ▪ To assess the impact of the plan on pupils' learning and achievement.
>
> ▪ To decide on how to disseminate successful new practices throughout the school.
>
> ▪ To make the process of reporting easier.

In most schools, the monitoring of INSET and the evaluation of its effectiveness and impact on classroom practice remain unsystematic. Even where these are undertaken, few schools use the results to inform their future planning. Too little attention is given to the impact such training has on classroom practice and on the raising of standards, and arrangements for dissemination are generally unsatisfactory.

OfSTED advises that schools need to consider:

- how to monitor INSET provision more closely and systematically

- how they might evaluate INSET, to determine its impact on improving subject teaching and raising standards of pupils' achievements

- giving greater attention to dissemination and to follow-up activity, to sustain the momentum of training, to broaden expertise and to share good practice

- making IT an INSET priority: teachers require sufficient familiarity with a range of IT facilities and the skill to apply these to the teaching of their subject

- the INSET needs of teachers and support assistants concerning provision for pupils with special educational needs, in order to help them deliver the teaching programmes devised for individual pupils.

Executive summary

- Within the context of school development, it is important to establish and provide for the learning needs and professional development of AUP practitioners.

- When planning, implementing and evaluating INSET programmes, the focus should be on the relevance of the programme to enhancing practitioner self-confidence in their ability to teach and manage the learning needs of all their pupils.

- All practitioners need support from a mentor when considering their professional development needs.

- Inclusive leadership is that which listens to and develops the voices of all groups in the community.

■ The full task of self-reflection and evaluation requires teachers to collaborate in decision-making that will transform their situation.

■ Self-development involves learning and understanding where you are within your job and career, seeing where you want to be and devising a coherent realisable plan in order to get there.

■ Support staff, e.g. TAs, require regular and effective CPD.

■ An AUP practitioner is a life-long learner.

■ Staff development includes personal, team and social development.

■ Evaluation is a component of development planning and prerequisite for preparing any subsequent plan.

Further reading

Blandford, S. (2004), *Professional Development Manual, 3rd Edition*, London: Pearson Education

Lunt, I. and Norwich, B. (1999), *Can Effective Schools be Inclusive Schools?*, London: Institute of Education

Slee, R., Tomlinson, S. and Weiner, G. (eds) (1998), *School effectiveness for whom? Challenges to the school effectiveness and school improvement movements*, London: Falmer Press

Tomlinson, H. (2004), *Educational leadership: personal growth for professional development*, London: Sage

Final Word

It is important that you take some time to reflect on the contents of this book in relation to your own practice – to gather thoughts and assess the knowledge and understanding gained. The following questions will help to critically view your position within an inclusive school community.

- What do you understand your role as an AUP practitioner to be?

- Is your voice and the voices of your colleagues, pupils, TAs and parents heard when decisions regarding school policy are being made?

- What is your vision for inclusion and how do you think it could be made real in your school community?

- What do you understand the current school community culture to be in relation to teaching and learning?

- What INSET have you experienced which enabled you to further understand the needs of all learners?

- In relation to meeting the needs of all your pupils what professional development do you need?

Inclusion is not to be viewed or understood as an end point or product that emerges when a teacher or school uses a particular formula for the management of teaching and learning. It is not a restricted scientific or modernist theory; inclusive thinking and practice results in a constant developmental process, where decisions are made and actions taken on the basis of inclusion – to be included. Such processes will result in the establishment of a learning community and a democratic school. Inclusion is not an easy option for a school community, it is the only option if schools and their communities are to progress in the current era. The following makes clear what inclusive educational practice is (Scottish Parliament, 2001, Col. 816):

> *The debate … is not about figures, politics or … dogma; it is about belief, faith, caring and the creation of community … It is about human rights and human beings.*

If practitioners are to continue valuing inclusive education, working towards the fuller development of their pupils and themselves, then a clear understanding of the theory and practice of inclusion is needed. Subsequent changes in practice need to be welcomed as enabling effective, inclusive teaching and learning that is celebrated within an inclusive school community.

References

Abberley, P. (1987), 'The concept of oppression and the development of a social theory of disability', *Disability, Handicap and Society*, 2(1): 5–19

Ainscow, M. (1988), 'Beyond the eyes of the monster: an analysis of recent trends in assessment and recording', *Support for Learning*, 3(3): 149–53

Ainscow, M. (1994), *Special Needs in the Classroom: A Teacher Education Guide*, London: Jessica Kingsley Publishers

Ainscow, M. (1995), 'Education for all: making it happen', *Support for Learning*, 10(4): 147–55

Ainscow, M. (1999), *Understanding the Development of Inclusive Schools*, London: Falmer Press

Ainscow, M. (2001), *Developing Inclusive Schools*, NFER bulletin, Issue 26, Slough: NFER

Ainscow, M. (ed.) (1991), *Effective Schools for All*, London: David Fulton Publishers

Allan, J. (2000), 'It's Good to Talk: Bridging the Gap between Disability Studies and Inclusive Education', *ISEC 2000 CD-ROM*, Oldham: Inclusive Consultancy and Training Ltd

Allan, J. (2003), 'Productive pedagogies and the challenge of Inclusion', *British Journal of Special Education*, 30(4): 175–9

Allan, J. and Cope, P. (2002), 'If you can: inclusion in music making presented at European Conference on Educational Research', *European Conference on Educational Research*, Lisbon, 11-14 September 2002

Allen-Knight, B. (1999), 'Towards inclusion of students with special educational needs in the regular classroom', *Support for Learning*, 14(1): 3–7

Arnold, J. (1964), *Slow Learners at School*, DES pamphlet No. 46, London: HMSO

Audit Commission (2002), *Special Education Needs: a mainstream issue*, London: Audit Commission

Avramedis, E., Bayliss, P. and Burden, R. (2000), 'A survey into mainstream teachers' attitudes towards the inclusion of children with special educational needs in the ordinary school in one local education authority', *Educational Psychology*, 20(2): 191–211

Baker, E., Wang, M. and Walberg, H. (1995), 'The effects of inclusion on learning', *Educational Leadership*, 52(4): 33–5

Ballard, K. (1995), 'Inclusion, paradigms, power and participation', in C. Clark, A. Dyson and A. Milward (eds), *Towards Inclusive Schools*, London: David Fulton Publishers

Barnes, C. (1996), *Disabling Imagery and the Media*, Leeds: Disability Press

Barton, L. (1997), 'Inclusive education: romantic, subversive or realistic?', *International Journal of Inclusive Education*, 1(3): 231–42

Barton, L. and Tomlinson, S. (eds) (1984), *Special Education and Social Interests*, London: Croom Helm

Bell, P. (1970), *Basic Teaching for Slow Learners*, London: Miller

Ben-Ari, R. and Shafir, D. (1988), *Social Integration in Elementary Schools*, Ramat-Gan, Israel: Institute for the Advancement of Social Integration in Schools, Bar-Ilan University

Bishop, A. and Jones, P. (2002), 'Promoting inclusive practice in primary initial teacher training: influencing hearts as well as minds', *Support for Learning*, 17(2): 58–62

Blamires, M. and Moore, J. (2004), *Support Services and Mainstream Schools*, London: David Fulton Publishers

Blandford, S. (1997), *Middle Management in Schools*, London: Pitman

Blandford, S. (1998), *Managing Discipline in Schools*, London: Routledge

Blandford, S. (2002), 'Organising a successful INSET day', *CPD Update Conference*, 11 March 2002

Blandford, S. (2003), *School Discipline Manual*, London: Pearson Education

Blandford, S. (2004), *Professional Development Manual*, 3rd Edition, London: Pearson Education

Blandford, S. and Blackburn, N. (2004), *School Financial Management Handbook*, London: Optimus

Blandford, S. and Duarte, S.J. (2002), 'Inclusion in the community', *European Conference on Educational Research*, Lisbon, 11–14 September 2002

Blandford, S. and Gibson, S. (2000), 'A poisoned chalice?', *Times Education Supplement*, August

Blandford, S. and Gibson, S. (2001), 'An examination of SEN management issues in England: a European Perspective', *European Conference on Educational Research*, University of Lille

Blanning, K. (2004), *What are the Makings of an Effective Teaching Assistant?* University of Plymouth: EDST214 Module

Bradbury, I., O'Neill, J. and West-Burnham, J. (2001), *Performance Management in Schools*, London: Pearson Education

Brennan, W. (1971), 'Policy for remedial education', *Remedial Education*, 6(1): 7–10

Brownlee, J. and Carrington, S. (2000), 'Opportunities for authentic experience and reflection: a teaching programme designed to change attitudes towards disability for pre-service teachers', *Support for Learning*, 15(3): 99–105

Burt, C. (1921), *Mental and Scholastic tests*, Oxford: Oxford University Press

Burt, C. (1935), *The Subnormal Mind*, Oxford: Oxford University Press

Burt, C. (1937), *The Backward Child*, London: Hodder and Stoughton

Bush, T. and Bell, L.A. (eds) (2002), *The Principles and Practice of Educational Management*, London: Paul Chapman Publishing

Caldwell, B.J. and Spinks, J.M. (1998), *Beyond the Self-Managing School*, London: Falmer Press

Carr, W. and Kemmis, S. (1986), *Becoming Critical: Education, Knowledge and Action Research*, Lewes: Falmer Press

Castelijns, J. (1996), 'Responsive instruction for young children: a study of how teachers can help easily distracted children become more attentive', *Emotional and Behavioural Difficulties*, 1(1), Spring

Centre for Studies on Inclusive Education (CSIE) (2000), *Index for Inclusion: developing learning and participation in schools*, Bristol: CSIE

Centre for Studies on Inclusive Education (CSIE) (2004), *Index for Inclusion: developing learning, participation and play in early years and childcare*, Bristol: CSIE

Cheminais, R. (2000), *Special Educational Needs for Newly Qualified Teachers*, London: David Fulton Publishers

Cheminais, R. (2004), 'Inclusive schools and classrooms', *SENCO Update*, May 2004, pp. 6–7, London: Optimus

Clark, C., Dyson, A. and Millward, A. (1995), *Towards Inclusive Schools*, London: David Fulton Publishers

Cline, T. (1992), 'Assessment of special educational needs: meeting reasonable expectation?', in T. Cline, (ed.), *The Assessment of Special Educational Needs: International Perspectives*, London: Routledge

Clough, P. and Barton, L. (eds) (1995), *Making Difficulties: Research and the Construction of Special Educational Needs*, London: Paul Chapman Publishing

Clough, P. and Barton, L. (eds) (1998), *Articulating with Difficulty: Research Voices in Special Education.* London: Paul Chapman Publishing

Coleman, M. and Bush, T. (1994), 'Managing with teams', in T. Bush and J. West-Burnham (eds), *The Principles of Educational Management*, Harlow: Longman

Cook, T. and Swain, J. (2001), 'Parents' perspectives on the closure of a special school: toward inclusion in partnership', *Educational Review*, 53(2): 192–8

Cook, T., Swain, J. and French, S. (2001), 'Voices from segregated schooling: towards an inclusive education system', *Disability and Society*, 16(2): 293–310

Corbett, J. (1994), 'Special language and political correctness', *British Journal of Special Education*, 21(1): 17–19

Corbett, J. (2001), *Supporting Inclusive Education: A Connective Pedagogy*, London: Falmer Press

Cornwall, J. and Tod, J. (1998), *IEPS: Emotional and Behavioural Difficulties*, London: David Fulton Publishers

Croll, P. and Moses, D. (1985), *One in Five*, London: Routledge

Croll, P. and Moses, D. (1998), 'Pragmatism, ideology and educational change: the case of special educational needs', *British Journal of Educational Studies*, 46: 11–25

Croll, P and Moses, D. (2003), 'Special educational needs across two decades: survey evidence from English primary schools', *British Educational Research Journal*, 29(5): 697–713

Department for Education (DfE) (1993), *Education Act*, London: HMSO

Department for Education (DfE) (1994a), *Code of Practice on the Identification and Assessment of Special Educational Needs*, London: HMSO

Department for Education (DfE) (1994b), Circular 2/94, *Local Management of Schools*, London: DfE

Department for Education (DfE) (1994c), *Circular 3/94, The Development of Special Schools*, London: DfE

Department for Education (DfE) (1994d), *Circular 6/94, The Organisation of Special Educational Provision*, London: DfE

Department for Education (DfE) (1994e), Circular 8/94, *Pupil Behaviour and Discipline*, London: DfE

Department for Education (DfE) (1994f), Circular 9/94, *The Education of Children with Emotional and Behavioural Difficulties*, London: DfE

Department for Education (DfE) (1994g), *Circular 10/94, Exclusions from School*, London: DfE

Department for Education (DfE) (1994h), *Circular 11/94, The Education by LEAs of Children Otherwise than at School*, London: DfE

Department for Education (DfE) (1994i), *Circular 12/94, The Education of Sick Children*, London: DfE

Department for Education (DfE) (1994j), *Circular 13/94, The Education of Children being looked after by Local Authorities*, London: DfE

Department for Education and Employment (DfEE) (1996), *The Senco Guide*, London: DfEE

Department for Education and Employment (DfEE), (1997), *Excellence for All Children. Meeting Special Educational Needs*, London: HMSO

Department for Education and Employment (DfEE) (1998), *Meeting Special Educational Needs: A Programme of Action*, London: HMSO

Department for Education and Skills (DfES) (2001a), *The Code of Practice for Special Educational Needs*, London: HMSO

Department for Education and Skills (DfES) (2001b), *School Action Plus*, London: HMSO

Department for Education and Skills (DfES) (2001c), *SEN Toolkit*, London: HMSO

Department for Education and Skills (DfES) (2003a), *Data Collection by Type of Special Educational Need*, London: HMSO

Department for Education and Skills (DfES) (2003b) *Key Stage Strategy*, London: HMSO

Department for Education and Skills (DfES) (2004a), *Barriers to Inclusion*, London: HMSO

Department for Education and Skills (DfES) (2004b), *Every Child Matters: Next Steps*, London: DfES Publications

Department for Education and Skills (DfES) (2004c), *The Management of SEN Expenditure (LEA/0149/2004)*, London: DfES Publications

Department for Education and Skills (DfES) (2004d), *Removing Barriers to Achievement: The Government's Strategy for SEN*, Nottingham: DfES Publications

Department of Education and Science (DES) (1965), *Circular 10/65*, London: DES

Department of Education and Science (DES) (1971), *Slow Learners in Secondary Schools*, Educational Survey 15, London: HMSO

Department of Education and Science (DES) (1980), *Special Needs in Education*, London: HMSO

Department of Education and Science (DES) (1981), *Education Act 'Special Educational Needs'*, London: HMSO

Department of Education and Science (DES) (1988), *Education Reform Act*, London: HMSO

Department of Education and Science (DES) (1990), *Special Educational Needs in Initial Teacher Training*, London: HMSO

Derrington, C. (1997), 'A Case for unpacking? Re-defining the role of the SENCO in the light of the CoP', *Support for Learning*, 12(3): 111–15

Dewey, J. (1960), *Democracy and Education – Introduction to the Philosophy of Education. Classics in World Literature*, Jerusalem: Hebrew University of Jerusalem and Bialik Institute (Hebrew translation)

Durkheim, E. (1967), *Education and Sociology*, New York: The Free Press

Dyson, A. and Gains, C. (1995), 'The role of the special needs co-ordinator: poisoned chalice or crock of gold', *Support for Learning*, 10(2): 50–6

Elliott, J., Bridges, D., Ebbutt, D., Gibson, R. and Nias, J. (1981), *School Accountability*, London: Grant McIntyre

Evans, J. and Lunt, I. (2002), 'Inclusive education: are there limits?', *European Journal of Special Needs Education*, 17(1): 1–14

Evidence for Policy and Practice Information and Co-ordinating Centre (EPPI) (2003), *How does collaborative Continuing Professional Development (CPD) for teachers of the 5–16 age range affect teaching and learning?*, London: Institute of Education

Farrell, P. (2000), 'The impact of research on developments in inclusive education', *International Journal of Inclusive Education*, 4: 153–62

Forest, M. and Pearpoint, J. (1992), 'MAPS: Action Planning', in J. Pearpoint, M. Forest and J. Shaw, *The Inclusion Papers: Strategies to Make Inclusion Work*, Toronto: Inclusion Press

Frederickson, N. and Cline, T. (2002), *Special Educational Needs, Inclusion and Diversity: a textbook*, Buckingham: Open University Press

Friedman, Y. (1986), *School, Home and Community in Israel, Alienation and Openness in the Educational Space*, Jerusalem: Henrietta Szold Institute (in Hebrew)

Garner, P. (1995), 'Sense or nonsense? Dilemmas in the SEN Code of Practice', *Support for Learning*, 10, 1, pp. 3-7

Garner, P. (1996a), 'Go forth and co-ordinate! What special needs co-ordinators think about the code of practice', *School Organisation*, 16(2): 170–86

Garner, P. (1996b), 'Student views on special educational needs courses in initial teacher education', *British Journal of Special Education*, 23(4): 176–90

Garner, P. (2000a), 'Mainstream teachers and inclusion. A chronic case of NIMSA (Not in My Subject Area)', *ISEC 2000 CD-ROM*, Oldham: Inclusive Consultancy and Training Ltd

Garner, P. (2000b), 'Pretzel only policy? Inclusion in the real world of initial teacher education', *British Journal of Special Education*, 27(3): 111–16

General Teaching Council (GTC) for England and Wales Trust (1993), *The Continuing Professional Development of Teachers*, London: GTC

Giangreco, M.F., Edelman, S., Cloniger, C. and Dennis, R. (1992), 'My Child has a classmate with severe disabilities: What parents of non-disabled children think about full inclusion', *Developmental Disabilities Bulletin*, 20(2): 1–12

Gibson, S. (1999), 'Determining the middle management role of the Special Educational Needs Co-ordinator in a secondary school setting within a pluralist society', *Graduate Education Forum*, 1(1): 14–29

Gibson, S. (2000), 'SENCO clustering – A practice developing within English secondary schools to aid inclusion', *ISEC 2000 CD-ROM*, Oldham: Inclusive Consultancy and Training Ltd

Gibson, S. (2001a), 'Middle management and the Special Educational Needs Co-ordinator (SENCO): a study of management in practice', PhD thesis, Oxford Brookes University

Gibson, S. (2001b), 'Managing the Code of Practice for Special Educational Needs. The inside story of the SENCO role', *British Educational Research Association Annual Conference*, University of Leeds.

Gibson, S. (2001c), *Special Educational Needs Teacher's Guide to the Internet*, Bristol: Classroom Resources

Gibson, S. (2002), 'The role of the SENCO in the mainstream secondary school setting. Implications for education management systems', *British Educational Research Association Annual Conference*, Exeter University

Gibson, S. (2003), 'The Learning Assistant Programme (LAP) – The merits of mentoring pupils with Behavioural, Emotional and Social Difficulties', *British Educational Research Association Annual Conference*, Herriott Watt University

Grace, G. (1998), 'Realizing the mission: catholic approaches to school effectiveness' in R. Slee, S. Tomlinson and G. Weiner (eds), *School Effectiveness for Whom? Challenges to the school effectiveness and school improvement movements*, London: Falmer Press

Gross, J. (2002), *Special Educational Needs in the Primary School: a practical guide*, Buckingham, Open University Press

Guaspari, R. (1999), *Music Of The Heart*, New York: Hyperion

Hall, V. and Oldroyd, D. (1990), *Management Self-development for Staff in Secondary Schools, Unit 2: Policy, Planning and Change*, Bristol: NDCEMP

Hargreaves, D.H. (1984), *Improving Secondary Schools*, London: ILEA

Harrison, B.T. (1995), 'Revaluing leadership and service in educational management' in: J. Bell and B.T. Harrison (eds), *Vision and Values in Managing Education*, London: David Fulton Publishers

Haynes, M.E. (1988), *Effective Meeting Skills*, London: Kogan Page

Hedge, N., Mole, R., LaGrave, J. and Cartwright, B. (1994), *Personal Communications at Work*, B600 The Capable Manager, Open Business School, Buckingham: Open University Press

Hegarty, S. (1987), *Meeting Special Needs in Ordinary Schools: An Overview*, London: Cassell

Hertz-Lazarowitz, R. and Miller, N. (1992), *Interaction in Cooperative Groups*, New York: Cambridge University Press

Hituv, M. (1989), 'The community school – principles, trends and methods of action', *Dapim*, 8: 83–87

Hornby, G. (1995), *Working with Parents of Children with Special Educational Needs*, London: Cassell

House, E. (1979), 'Technology versus craft: a ten-year perspective on innovation', *Curriculum Studies*, 11(1): 1–15

Hoy, W. and Miskel, C. (1991), *Educational Administration: Theory, Research and Practice*, New York: McGraw-Hill

Hurt, W. (1988), *Outside the Mainstream*, London: Batsford

Inglese, J. (1996), 'Special Teachers? Perceptions of the special expertise required for effective special educational needs teaching and advisory work', *Support for Learning*, 11(2): 83–7

Johnson, B., Whitington, V. and Oswald, M. (1994), 'Teachers' views on school discipline: a theoretical framework', *Cambridge Journal of Education*, 24(2): 261–76

Jones, N. (ed.) (1989), *School Management and Pupil Behaviour*, Lewes: Falmer Press

Jowett, S. and Baginsky, M. (1988), 'Parents and education: a survey of their involvement and discussion of some issues', *Educational Research*, 30, pp. 36-45

Katz, D. and Kahn, R.L. (1978), *The Social Psychology of Organisations*, New York: John Wiley

Kelley-Laine, K. (1998), 'Parents as partners in schooling: The current state of affairs', *Childhood Education*, 74(6): 342–5

Kenworthy, J. and Whittaker, J. (2000), 'Anything to declare? The struggle for inclusive education and children's rights', *Disability and Society*, 15(2): 219–31

Lacey, P. (2001), *Support Partnerships: Collaboration in Action*, London: David Fulton Publishers

Lawson, H. (2002), 'Effective target setting', *Special*, Spring, pp. 18–19

Lewis, A. (1995a), 'Policy shifts concerning special needs provisions in mainstream primary schools', *British Journal of Educational Studies*, 43(3): 318–32

Lewis, A. (1995b), *Children's Understanding of Disability*, London: Routledge

Lewis, A. and Lindsay, G. (eds) (2000), *Researching Children's Perspectives*, Buckingham: Open University Press

Lewis, A. and Neill, S. (1996), 'How is it for you?', *Special Children*, 92: 7–8

Lewis, A., Neill, S.J. and Campbell, R.J. (1996), *The Implementation of the Code of Practice in Primary and Secondary schools*, London: National Union of Teachers/University of Warwick

Lewis, A., Neill, S. and Campbell, J. (1997), 'SENCOs and the Code: a national survey', *Support for Learning*, 12(1): 3–9

Lewis, A. and Norwich, B. (2001), *Do Pupils with Learning Difficulties need Teaching Strategies that are Different from Those used with Other Pupils?*, NFER bulletin, Issue 26, Slough: NFER

Lewis, A. and Norwich, B. (2004), *Special Teaching for Special Children*, Buckingham: Open University Press

Lindsay, G. and Thompson, D. (eds) (1997), *Values into Practice in Special Education*, London: David Fulton Publishers

Lipsky, D. and Gartner, A. (1995), 'The evaluation of inclusive education programs', *Bulletin of National Centre on Educational Restructuring and Inclusion*, 2: 1–9

Lipsky, D. and Gartner, A. (1996), 'Inclusion, school restructuring and the remaking of American society', *Harvard Educational Review*, 66(4), pp. 1–32, http//www.edreview.org/harvard96/1996w96gart.htm

Lipsky, D. and Gartner, A. (1998), 'Taking inclusion into the future', *Educational Leadership*, 56(2): 78–81

Lunt, I. and Norwich, B. (1999), *Can Effective Schools be Inclusive Schools?*, London: Institute of Education

Machter, E. (2000), *Parents' Involvement in Community Schools in Israel: Patterns, Motives & Expectations*, Oxford: Oxford Brookes University/Westminster Institute of Education

Male, D.B. and May, D.S. (1997), 'Stress, burnout and workload in teachers of children with special educational needs', *British Journal of Special Education*, 24(3): 133–40

Male, J. (1997), *Children First: A guide to the needs of disabled children in school*, London: RADAR

Marshall, J., Ralph, S. and Palmer, S. (2002), 'I wasn't trained to work with them: mainstream teachers' attitudes to children with speech and language difficulties', *International Journal of Inclusive Education*, 6(3): 199–215

Mintzberg, H. (1983), *Power in and around Organisations*, New Jersey: Prentice-Hall

Mittler, P. (1993), *Teacher Education for Special Educational Needs*, Tamworth: NASEN

Mittler, P. (2000), *Working Towards Inclusive Education: Social Contexts*, London: David Fulton Publishers

Moll, L.C. and Whitmore, K.F. (1998), 'Vygotsky in classroom practice: moving from individual transmission to social transaction', in D. Faulkner, K. Littleton and M. Woodhead (eds), *Learning Relationships in the Classroom*, London: Routledge

Mortimore, P., Sammons, P., Stoll, L., Lewis, D. and Ecob, R. (1988), *School Matters: The Junior Years*, Salisbury: Open Books

Munby, S. (1994), 'Assessment and pastoral care: sense, sensitivity and standards', in R. Best, P. Lang, C. Lodge and C. Watkins (eds), *Pastoral Care and Personal-Social Education: Entitlement and Provision*, London: Cassell

Musgrave, P.W. (1968), *Society and Education since 1800*, London: Methuen

Nakken, H. and Jan Pijl, S. (2002), 'Getting along with classmates in regular schools: a review of the effects of integration on the development of social relationships', *International Journal of Inclusive Education*, 6(1): 47–61

National Policy Board for Educational Administration (NPBEA) (1993), *Principles for our Changing Schools*, Virginia: NPBEA

National Society for the Prevention of Cruelty to Children (NSPCC) (2001), *Two Way Street: Communicating with disabled children and young people*, Leicester: NSPCC

Nind, M., Rix, J., Sheehy, K. and Simmons, K. (eds) (2003), *Inclusive Education: Diverse Perspectives*, London: David Fulton Publishers

Norwich, B. (1996), 'Special needs education or education for all', *British Journal of Special Education*, 23(3): 79

Norwich, B. (1997), *A Trend Towards Inclusion*, Bristol: CSIE

Norwich, B. (ed.) (2000), *Specialist Teaching for Special Educational Needs and Inclusion*, Tamworth: NASEN

Norwich, B. and Daniels, H. (1997), 'Teacher support teams for special educational needs in primary schools: evaluating a teacher-focused support scheme', *Educational Studies*, 23(1): 5–24

Norwich, B. and Kelly, N. (2004), 'Pupils' views on inclusion: moderate learning difficulties and bullying in mainstream and special schools', *British Educational Research Journal*, 30(1): 43–65

Norwich, B. and Lewis, A. (2001), 'A critical review of evidence concerning teaching strategies for pupils with special educational needs', *British Educational Research Journal*, 27(3): 313–29

Noy, B. (1984), *Parent Participation in the Educational Work of the School*, Jerusalem, Emanuel Yaffe College for Senior Teachers (in Hebrew)

Office for Standards in Education (OfSTED) (1995), *Preparing for Inspection*, London: OfSTEAD Publications.

Office for Standards in Education (OfSTED) (1999), *The SEN Code of Practice: three years on*, London: HMI

Office for Standards in Education (OfSTED (2000), *Evaluating Educational Inclusion*, London: HMI

Office for Standards in Education (OfSTED) (2004a), *Setting Targets for Pupils with Special Educational Needs*, London: OfSTED Publications

Office for Standards in Education (OfSTED) (2004b), *Special Educational Needs and Disability, HMI 2276*, London: OfSTED Publications

Oliver, M. (1988), 'The social and political context of educational policy: the case of special needs', in L. Barton (ed.), *The Politics of Special Educational Needs*, London: Falmer Press

Oliver, M. (1998), *Disabled People and Social Policy*, London: Longman

Ormston, M. (1996), *Leadership and Leadership Qualities*, Oxford: Oxford Brookes University, School of Education

Ormston, M. and Shaw, M. (1993) *Mentoring*, Oxford: Oxford Brookes University, School of Education

Peck, C., Donaldson, J. and Pezzoli, M. (1990), 'Some benefits non-handicapped adolescents perceive for themselves from their social relationships with peers who have severe handicaps', *Journal of the Association for Persons with Severe Handicaps*, 15(4): 241–9

Peetsma, T., Vergreer, M., Roeleveld, J. and Karsten, S. (2001), 'Inclusion in education: comparing pupils' development in special and regular education', *Educational Review*, 53(2): 126–35

Pike, N. (1996), 'Expenditure fear over special help', *Times Educational Supplement*, 29 November

Poster, C. (1982), *Community Education*, London: Heinemann

Potts, P. (1982), *Special Needs in Education*, Buckingham: Open University Press

Prawat, R.S. and Nickerson, J.R. (1985), 'The relationship between teacher thought and action and student affective outcomes', *The Elementary School Journal*, 85: 529–40

Ramasut, A. and Reynolds, D. (1993), 'Developing effective whole-school approaches to special educational needs: from school effectiveness to school development practice', in R. Slee (ed.), *Is There a Desk With My Name on it? The Politics of Integration*, London: Falmer Press

Raywid, M.A. (1984), 'Synthesis of research on schools of choice', *Educational Leadership*, 41(7): 70–8

Rea, J. and Weiner, G. (1998), 'Cultures of blame and redemption – when empowerment becomes control: practitioners' views of the effective schools movement', in R. Slee, G. Weiner and S. Tomlinson (eds), *School Effectiveness for Whom?: Challenges to the school effectiveness and the school improvement movements*, London: Falmer Press

Reynolds, D. (1995), 'Using school effectiveness knowledge for children with special needs – the problems and possibilities' in C. Clark, A. Dyson and A. Millward (eds), *Towards Inclusive Schools*, London: David Fulton Publishers

Reynolds, D. (1997), 'School effectiveness: retrospect and prospect', *Scottish Educational Review*, 29(2): 87–113

Roberts, H. (2000), 'Listening to children and hearing them', in P. Christensen and A. James (eds), *Research with Children: Perspectives and Practices*, London: Falmer Press

Robinson, T. (1997), *Coping with Kids: Assertive Discipline for Parents*, UK Leader's Manual, Bristol: Behaviour Management

Rogers, W.A. (1996), *Managing Teacher Stress*, London: Pitman

Rose, R. (2001), 'Primary school teacher perceptions of the conditions required to include pupils with special educational needs', *Educational Review*, 53(2): 147–56

Rosenthal, H. (2001), 'Discussion paper – working towards inclusion: I am another other', *Educational Psychology in Practice*, 17(4): 386–92

Rouse, M. and Agbenu, R. (1998), 'Assessment and special educational needs: teachers' dilemmas', *British Journal of Special Education*, 25(2): 81–7

Rouse, M. and Florian, L. (1996), 'Effective inclusive schools: a study in two countries', *Cambridge Journal of Education*, 26(1): 71–85

Russell, P. (1997), 'Parents as partners: some early impressions of the impact of the Code of Practice', in S. Wolfendale (ed.), *Working with Parents of SEN Children After the Code of Practice*, London: David Fulton Publishers

Rutter, M., Maughan, B., Mortimore, P. and Ouston, J. (1979), *Fifteen Thousand Hours: Secondary Schools and Their Effects on Children*, London: Open Books

Sandow, S. (ed.) (1994), *Whose Special Need?* London: Paul Chapman Publishing

Schonell, F. (1924), *Backwardness in the Basic Subjects*, London: Oliver and Boyd

Scottish Executive (2004), *Children's Charter*, Edinburgh: Scottish Executive

Scottish Parliament (2001), *Official Report of Debate on Motion S1M-1931: Special Educational Needs*

Sebba, J. and Sachdev, D. (1997), *What Works in Inclusive Education?*, Ilford: Barnardo's

Senge, P.M. (1990), *The Fifth Discipline: The Art and Practice of the Learning Organization*, New York: Doubleday

Serow, R.C. and Solomon, D. (1979), 'Classroom climates and students' inter group behaviour', *Journal of Educational Psychology*, 71: 669–76

Sharron, H. (2003), 'Total inclusion, total school improvement', *Managing Schools Today*, September/October

Shevlin, M. and O'Moore, M. (2000), 'Fostering positive attitudes: reactions of mainstream pupils to contact with their counterparts who have severe/profound intellectual disabilities', *European Journal of Special Needs Education*, 15(2): 206–17

Skrtic, T.M. (1991), 'The special education paradigm: equity as the way to excellence', *Harvard Educational Review*, 61(2): 148–201

Skrtic, T.M. (1999), 'Learning disabilities as organisational pathologies', in R.J. Sternberg and L. Spear-Swirling (eds), *Perspectives on Learning Disabilities*, Oxford: Westview

Slee, R. (1998), 'The politics of theorising special education', in C. Clark, A. Dyson and A. Millward (eds), *Theorising Special Education*, London: Routledge

Slee, R. (2001), 'Inclusion in practice: does practice make perfect?', *Educational Review*, 53(2): 113–22

Slee, R., Tomlinson, S. and Weiner, G. (eds) (1998), *School Effectiveness for Whom? Challenges to the school effectiveness and school improvement movements*, London: Falmer Press

Smedley, B. (1974), 'Organisation of remedial education in the secondary school', *Remedial Education*, 9(3): 117–21

Solity, J. (1992), *Special Education*, London: Cassell

Stainback, S., Stainback, W., Esat, K. and Sapon-Shevin, M. (1994), 'A commentary on inclusion and the development of positive self-identity by people with disabilities', *Exceptional Children*, 60: 486–90

Stakes, R. and Hornby, G. (1997), *Change in Special Education*, London: Cassell

Staub, D. and Peck, C.A. (1994), 'What are the outcomes for non-disabled pupils?', *Educational Leadership*, 52(4): 36–40

Stein, M. and Harpaz, Y. (1995), *The Community School: Symposium*, Jerusalem: ACYSC/The Administration of Community Education School (in Hebrew)

Stoll, L. (1991), 'School effectiveness and school improvement', in J. White and M. Barber (eds), *Perspectives on School Effectiveness and School Improvement*, London: Institute of Education

Tansley, A. and Culliford, R. (1960), *The Education of the Slow Learning Child*, London: Routledge and Keegan Paul

Tarr, J. and Thomas, G. (1996), *The Monitoring and Evaluation of Schools' SEN Policies*, Bristol: University of the West of England

Teacher Training Agency (TTA) (1998), *National Standards for SENCOs*, London: TTA

Thomas, G. (1997), 'Inclusive schools for an inclusive society', *British Journal of Special Education*, 24(3): 103–7

Thomas, G. and Loxley, A. (2001), *Deconstructing Special Education and Constructing Inclusion*, Buckingham: Open University Press

Thomas, G. and Vaughan, M. (2004), *Inclusive Education*, Buckingham: Open University Press

Thomas, G., Walker, D. and Webb, J. (1998), *The Making of the Inclusive School*, London: Routledge

Thompson, M. (1997), 'Response to the TTA's consultation on the "National Standards for SENCOs"', *Education-line*, October, available at www.leeds.ac.uk/educol

Tilstone, C., Florian, L. and Rose, R. (eds) (1998), *Promoting Inclusive Practice*, London: Routledge

Tod, J. (2004), 'Removing barriers to achievement: changing the role of the SENCO', *SENCO Update*, June 2004, pp. 4–5, London: Optimus

Tod, J., Powell, S., Cornwall, J., Soan S. and Burroughs, L. (2004), *Behaviour Management: A Systematic Review of How Theories Explain Learning Behaviour in School Contexts*, Canterbury: CCCUC/TTA

Tomlinson, H. (2004), *Educational Leadership: personal growth for professional development*, London: Sage

Tomlinson, S. (1982), *A Sociology of Special Education*, London: Routledge and Keegan Paul

Uditsky, B. (1993), 'From integration to inclusion: the Canadian experience', in R. Slee (ed.) *Is There a Desk With My Name on It? The Politics of Integration*, London: Falmer Press

United Nations (1989), *The Convention on the Rights of the Child: Adopted by the General Assembly of the United Nations*, 20 November.

United Nations Educational, Scientific and Cultural Organisation (UNESCO), (1994) *World Conference on Special Needs Education: Access and Quality*, Paris: UNESCO

Vincent, C. (2004), *Including Parents*, Buckingham: Open University Press

Vincent, C., Evans, J., Lunt, I. and Young, P. (1995), 'Policy and practice: the changing nature of special educational provision in schools', *British Educational Research Journal*, 22(1): 4–11

Vygotsky, L.S. (1962), *Thought and Language*, edited and translated by E. Hanfmann and G. Vakar. Cambridge, New York: MIT Press

Warnock, M. (1978), *Report of the Committee of Enquiry into the Education of Handicapped Children and Young People*, London: HMSO

Warnock, M. (1982), 'Children with special needs in ordinary schools: integration revisited', *Education Today*, 32(2): 56–62

West-Burnham, J. (1997), *Managing Quality in Schools*, London: Pearson Education

Westwood, P. (1975), *The Remedial Teacher's Handbook*, London: Oliver and Boyd

White, R. and Lippitt, R. (1983), 'Leadership behaviour and member reactions in three social climates', in D. Cartwright and A. Zander (eds), *Group Dynamics*, London: Tavistock Publishing

Wright, D. (1971), *The Psychology of Moral Behaviour*, London: Penguin

Index

Added to a page number, 't' denotes a table.